How to Prepare For the STATE STANDARDS

VOL. 2

teacher

4th Grade Edition

By Nancy Samuels

carney
EDUCATIONAL SERVICES

CARNEY EDUCATIONAL SERVICES
Helping Students Help Themselves

Special thanks to Rim Namkoong, our illustrator

This book is dedicated to:

The moms and dads who get up early and stay up late. You are the true heroes, saving our future, one precious child at a time.

All the kids who don't make the evening news. To the wide-eyed children, full of love, energy, and wonder. You are as close to perfection as this world will ever see.

TABLE OF CONTENTS

Introduction for Parents

The Focus and Purpose of this Book

Many states have recently adopted rigorous academic content standards for students in grades K – 12. The content standards set forth exactly what students need to learn in each grade level in language arts, mathematics, history-social science, and science. This book presents exercises that test student mastery of each of the academic content standards.

In conjunction with the standards, many states have initiated the standardized testing programs. As a part of these programs, students take nationally normed achievement tests designed by the state to assess how well the students have mastered the skills and information covered in the state standards. The results give teachers, parents, and students invaluable information about a child's relative academic strengths and the next steps for learning.

The purpose of this book is twofold: (1) to assist students in mastering the information addressed in each of the content standards, and (2) to prepare students to perform their best on the appropriate standardized test. It is designed for student use in the classroom or for support of classroom lessons. The book is divided into "practice skill" sections that correlate to the various strands of the content standards. Each section is introduced with a statement of expectations for student learning in the practice skill area. Every section also contains tips and strategies to help the student learn the information or reason through the exercises. The exercises are presented in various formats that will give the students practice in answering questions much like those that they are likely to encounter on any standardized nationally normed achievement test.

Academic Content Standards in Grade 4

By the end of grade 4, students are expected to achieve mastery in several areas. The major areas of focus are listed below.

LANGUAGE ARTS areas of focus include:
- Word Analysis, Fluency, and Systematic Vocabulary Development
  - Read aloud fluently and with expression
  - Use root words and word origins to determine the meaning of unknown words
  - Understand and use antonyms, synonyms, and idioms
  - Know roots and affixes from Greek and Latin and use them to analyze the meaning of complex words
  - Distinguish and interpret words with multiple meanings
  - Explain the figurative and metaphorical use of words in context
- Reading Comprehension (Focus on Informational Materials)
  - Use text features (format, sequence, charts, maps, etc.)
  - Analyze text organization (sequential or chronological order, compare and contrast, cause and effect, proposition and support)

- o Make and confirm predictions about text
- o Distinguish between cause and effect and between fact and opinion in text
- o Follow multi-step instructions in a basic technical manual
- Literary Response and Analysis
  - o Describe the structural differences in various forms of literature, including fantasies, fables, myths, legends, and fairy tales
  - o Identify the main events of the plot, their causes, and the influence of each event on future actions
  - o Use knowledge of situation, setting, and of character's traits and motivations to determine the causes for that character's actions
  - o Understand that "theme" refers to the meaning or moral of a selection and recognize themes in sample works
  - o Identify figurative language in literary works
- Listening and Speaking
  - o Listen critically and ask thoughtful questions
  - o Respond to relevant questions with elaboration
  - o Summarize major ideas and supporting evidence presented in spoken messages and formal presentations
  - o Give precise directions and instructions
  - o Present effective introductions and conclusions in oral presentations
  - o Convey information using a variety of traditional structures (cause and effect, similarity and difference, and posing and answering a question)
  - o Use details, examples, anecdotes, or experiences to explain or clarify
  - o Deliver quality narrative presentations, informative presentations
- Writing Strategies and Applications
  - o Write clear, coherent sentences and paragraphs that develop a central idea
  - o Use a thesaurus to enhance written expression
  - o Use various reference materials
  - o Work through the writing process of prewriting, drafting, revising, and editing. Revise manuscripts to improve meaning and focus
  - o Create multiple-paragraph compositions that contain an introductory paragraph; establish and support a central idea with a topic sentence; include supporting paragraphs with simple facts, details, and explanations; and conclude with a summary paragraph
  - o Write narratives that relate ideas, observations, or recollections of an event or experience
  - o Write responses to literature that demonstrate an understanding of a literary work. Support judgments through specific references.
  - o Write information reports framed by a central question about an issue or situation
  - o Write summaries that contain the main ideas of the reading selection and the most significant details
- Written and Oral English Language Conventions
  - o Use simple and compound sentences in writing and speaking
  - o Combine short, related sentences with appositives, participial phrases, adjectives, adverbs, and prepositional phrases

o Identify and correctly use verbs, adverbs, prepositions, and coordinating conjunctions in writing and speaking
o Use correct capitalization, punctuation, and spelling

MATHEMATICS areas of focus include:
- Number Sense
  o Read and write whole numbers in the millions
  o Order and compare whole numbers and decimals to two decimal places
  o Round whole numbers through the millions to various place values
  o Explain fractions and equivalents of fractions
  o Write tenths and hundredths in decimal and fraction notations and know common fraction and decimal equivalents
  o Identify the relative position of positive fractions, mixed numbers, and decimals
  o Add and subtract decimals to two places
  o Add, subtract, multiply, and divide multidigit numbers
  o Factor small whole numbers and identify prime numbers to 13
  o Apply mathematical procedures to solving problems
- Algebra and Functions
  o Use symbols to stand for a number in simple expressions or equations
  o Interpret and evaluate mathematical expressions that use parentheses
  o Use and interpret formulas to answer questions (find area, etc.)
  o Understand that an equation such as $y = 3x + 5$ is a prescription for determining a second number when a first number is given
  o Know that equals added to equals are equal, and that equals multiplied by equals are equal
- Measurement and Geometry
  o Understand and compute perimeter and area for rectangles, squares, and any combination of those figures
  o Use two-dimensional coordinate grids to represent points and graph lines and simple figures
  o Identify parallel and perpendicular lines, and the radius and diameter of a circle
  o Identify congruent figures and those with bilateral and rotational symmetry
  o Identify various types of angles
  o Identify various types of geometric solids and how they can be interpreted in two dimensional models for construction
  o Know the definitions of different triangles and quadrilaterals, and identify their attributes
- Statistics, Data Analysis, and Probability
  o Collect and chart different data sets
  o Identify the mode and any outliers for numerical data sets
  o Interpret two-variable data graphs to answer questions about a situation
  o Represent all possible outcomes for a simple probability situation in an organized way (table, grid, tree diagram)

- Express outcomes of experimental probability situation verbally and numerically
- Mathematical Reasoning
  - Make decisions about how to set up a problem; use appropriate problem solving strategies
  - Analyze problems by identifying relationships, distinguishing relevant from irrelevant information, sequencing and prioritizing information, and observing patterns
  - Use estimation to verify the reasonableness of calculated results

HISTORY-SOCIAL SCIENCE areas of focus include:

- Places and Regions on a Map
  - Use latitude and longitude to determine locations

STATE REPORT
- State History Report reviews key facts about the student's state of residence and the state's local history.
- Review of key persons in the student's state history, timeline of major events and geographic make up of the state.
- Student uses research sources such as encyclopedia or Internet sites to attain information to complete the report.
- Create original sketches and drawing to represent key state symbols such as the state flag, tree and flower.

BIOGRAPHY REPORT
- Complete an original biography of an important person in the student's state history.

SCIENCE areas of focus include:

- Physical Sciences
  - o Understand that electricity and magnetism are related effects that have many useful applications in everyday life
  - o Design and build simple series and parallel circuits
  - o Build a simple compass and use it to detect magnetic effects
  - o Build a simple electromagnet
  - o Discuss electrical energy
- Life Sciences
  - o Describe ecosystems and the relationships in food chains and food webs
  - o Discuss the roles of producers and consumers
  - o Discuss how living organisms depend on one another and on their environment for survival
  - o Understand the role of microorganisms
  - o Describe the interactions between plants and animals
- Earth Sciences
  - o Understand how rocks and minerals reflect the processes that formed them
  - o Differentiate among the various types of rocks by referring to their properties and methods of formation
  - o Identify rock-forming minerals
  - o Describe how waves, wind, water, and ice shape and reshape Earth's land surface
  - o Describe erosion, landslides, volcanic eruptions, and earthquakes

Subjects Tested on Standardized Tests in Grade 4

Students in grade 4 are tested in language arts and mathematics. The language arts portion of the test includes questions that measure reading vocabulary (synonyms, multiple meanings, determining word meanings in context), reading comprehension (textual, recreational, and functional materials) and process (making inferences, extending meaning through predictions), spelling, and language (elements of grammar, capitalization, punctuation, usage, sentence structure, content, and organization), study skills (dictionary, library, and reference skills), and information skills (locating information and using textual features). The math sections of the test measure student mastery of the same concepts that are the focus of the academic content standards: number sense, math facts and procedures, whole number computation, fraction and decimal concepts, geometry and measurement, patterns and relationships, statistics and probability, mathematical reasoning, and problem solving strategies.

Test Taking Strategies for Students in Grade 4

Students in grade 4 receive their own test booklets in which to read the questions and a separate answer sheet for filling in a bubble next to their answer choice. The bubbling marks are the only ones that they will be allowed to make on the tests. For the math sections, however, students may use scratch paper. No calculators are allowed. In fact, to ensure the integrity of the testing, during the testing period teachers must remove all charts and diagrams relevant to the subject of the test.

►Listen Carefully, Bubble Accurately, and Keep Up With the Pace

An important aspect of the test is that a student must listen carefully and pay close attention to the teacher before, during, and after the test. The teacher will give oral instructions about the test. The teacher's words are scripted, and the script sets strict limits on the number of times instructions and test questions may be repeated. A student must remain attentive, keep track of the number of the question that s/he is answering, and make sure to keep up with the pace.

►Eliminate Any Unreasonable Answer Choices and Select the Best Answer

In a test with a multiple-choice format, it is sometimes difficult to find the "perfect" answer among the choices given. The first thing to do is eliminate all obviously wrong choices. Concentrate on the remaining ones. Ultimately, it may be difficult to choose between two choices. In such instances, the student should reread the question carefully. It will likely contain key words needed to select the best answer. It may be the case that two choices are factually correct, but one choice more directly answers the question than another. Consider the following example.

Read the passage. Answer the question about it.

Dogs are members of the canine family. They come in a variety of breeds and hundreds of different shapes and sizes. Each breed has its own special talent. Sheep dogs herd cattle and sheep. Golden retrievers make good guide dogs for the blind. St. Bernards are famous for rescuing people in the mountains. Huskies pull sleds to transport people and supplies over frozen terrain.

1. What is the main idea of this selection?

    a. All dogs are canines.
    b. All dogs look the same.
    c. Dogs make good companions.
    d. Different dog breeds have special talents.

To select the best answer, first eliminate the obviously incorrect choice "b." Although the remaining choices are all true statements, and even though choice "a" is taken directly from the selection, only choice "d" addresses the main idea of the passage. Choice "d" is the best answer.

►Solve Math Problems on Scratch Paper. Work Neatly and Keep Organized.

Students may not make marks in the test booklet. Teachers will distribute scratch paper for solving problems. It will be important to transfer the problem accurately onto the scratch paper, align columns, and keep track of what problem is being solved. This means that the student will need to pay extra attention to neatness, organization, and accuracy. Time is often a factor in math tests, so it is will be necessary to work steadily and focus on the task at hand. If the student is really stumped on one problem, it may be best to give an educated guess, make a notation about the problem number, and return to it later if time permits. If you skip a problem, be sure to skip the corresponding bubble on the answer sheet, as well. Any questions left unanswered will be counted wrong, so it is best not too spend too much time on any one problem. There is probably a question waiting down the line that will be much easier to solve!

Introduction for Students

About This Book

Your state has developed a set of guidelines (called "academic content standards") for students in every grade, from Kindergarten through grade 12. These standards tell us exactly what students need to learn in each grade level in language arts, math, history-social science (social studies), and science. The exercises in this book follow the standards for fourth grade. As you complete these exercises, you will be able to tell which standards you have learned and which areas you might want to review.

In order to know how well children are learning the information they need to know, all students take certain tests every year usually in the spring. In fourth grade, students take tests in language arts and math. The exercises in this book will help you get ready for these tests. They will give you practice in answering questions about the things that you will need to know by the end of fourth grade.

This book is divided into four sections, one for each of the subjects where there are established standards: language arts, math, history-social science, and science. Each section is divided into practice skill areas that explain what students are expected to know within the particular standard. Look for the box of tips in each section. The tips will explain special ways to remember the information, or will give you help in working through the exercises.

What You Will Learn in the Fourth Grade

In the fourth grade you will accomplish many things. Here are some of them.

Language Arts - You will read silently and read aloud various works of literature. You will use your knowledge of word origins and word relationships, as well as historical and literary context clues to learn the meaning of many new words. You will analyze poetry, stories, and books that give you new information. You will discern main ideas and concepts presented in your textbooks, and draw inferences, conclusions, or generalizations about what you read. You will organize your thoughts to speak and write in various genres about various topics in a way that is clear to others. You will write sentences and paragraphs that develop a central idea, eventually creating multiple-paragraph compositions.

Math – You will work with numbers from 1,000,000 to 0.01. You will compute with multidigit numbers (including addition and subtraction of decimals), and learn the relationships between decimals and fractions. You will use variables in simple expressions and equations, and learn how to factor whole numbers. Working with algebraic principles, you will manipulate equations. In measurement and geometry, you will find the perimeter and area of rectangles and squares, and work with various triangles. Statistics, data analysis, and probability will be part of your studies. You will develop a series of strategies and skills to help you solve all types of math problems.

History-Social Studies – Fourth grade students study the development of their state from pre-Columbian times to the present. Students examine the state in the context of the rest of the nation. They also study the U.S. Constitution, key principles of their state Constitution, and the roles and responsibilities of federal, state, and local governments.

Science – One area of focus in the physical sciences is the study of the relationship between electricity and magnetism. In the life sciences, you will study various ecosystems and the relationship between the plant and animal worlds. Fourth grade students also study rocks, minerals, water, and the ways that the Earth's land surface is shaped and reshaped. In learning about these topics, you will question, observe, predict, investigate, experiment, and record data. You will be a scientist!

Test Taking Tips

1. **Read for 20 minutes every day.** The skills that you use to read are the same skills that will help you to do well on any test.

2. **Review a little every day.** If you practice or review what you have already learned in class, it will help you to remember the information when it appears on a test. It is easier and more effective to learn something in six 10-minute sessions that in one hour-long session.

3. **When solving math problems, work neatly and keep organized.** Take extra care when you are writing problems or transferring answers from scratch paper to an answer column or test booklet. You must copy the problems accurately and compute accurately. It helps to work each problem in its own area, separated from another problem. Be sure to align columns correctly. This will help you to avoid careless errors.

4. **Stay focused.** Often, you will only have limited time to complete a test. Other times you will need to listen to oral instructions or respond to what you hear. Be sure to concentrate on the task at hand. Keep working and don't let your mind wander. If you don't know an answer, be

sure not to spend so much time on that one question that you can't finish the rest of the test. Consider taking an educated guess or skipping the question and coming back to work on it after you have completed the rest of the test.

5.   In multiple-choice tests, eliminate obviously wrong choices and select the best answer. Sometimes it is difficult to find the "perfect" answer among the choices given. The first thing to do is eliminate the choices that are obviously wrong and concentrate on the remaining ones. If you find it difficult to choose between two choices that both seem correct, go back and reread the question very carefully. Look for key words that will help you focus on the best choice. Don't be fooled by choices that are true, but that do not directly answer the question! Here is an example:

Read the passage and answer the question about it.

Dogs are members of the canine family. They come in a variety of breeds and hundreds of different shapes and sizes. Each breed has its own special talent. Sheep dogs herd cattle and sheep. Golden retrievers make good guide dogs for the blind. St. Bernards are famous for rescuing people in the mountains. Huskies pull sleds to transport people and supplies over frozen terrain.

1. What is the main idea of this selection?

    a. All dogs are canines.
    b. All dogs look the same.
    c. Dogs make good companions.
    d. Different dog breeds have special talents.

To select the best answer, first eliminate the obviously incorrect choice "b." Although the remaining choices are all true statements, and even though choice "a" is stated in the paragraph, only choice "d" tells the main idea of the paragraph. Choice "d" is the correct answer.

6.   Take some practice tests so you won't be nervous. The more you get used to thinking about what you know and answering questions about it, the more comfortable and confident you can be. A positive attitude is always the best way to approach learning and testing. The exercises in this book are designed to help you learn what you need to know in the fourth grade and to practice answering questions about it. You will be able to say, "I know how to do this. I do it all the time!"

LANGUAGE ARTS

Practice Skill: READING VOCABULARY - SYNONYMS

Expectation: Identify words that have similar meanings.

> Tip: Synonyms are words that mean the same as other words. Knowing many synonyms for words will make your writing more interesting and will help you explain exactly what you mean. For example, instead of big house, you might use villa, mansion, estate, or castle. Each one brings a different picture to the reader's mind. Use a thesaurus to help you find synonyms and use just the right word in your writing.

Select a synonym to match the <u>underlined</u> word.

Example: He was <u>grateful</u> for their kind words.

    a. embarrassed
    b. appreciative
    c. upset
    d. regretful

The correct answer is *b*. *Appreciative* is a synonym for *grateful*, and substituting one word for the other does not significantly change the meaning of the sentence.

1. After three days stranded in the desert, they were in <u>dire</u> need of water.

    a. extreme
    b. casual
    c. probable
    d. free

2. The first pioneers had to cross miles of <u>desolate</u> territory on foot.

    a. lush
    b. barren
    c. harsh
    d. treacherous

3. She is so <u>ingenious</u> that she could design a mousetrap from a toothpick and string.

    a. smart
    b. funny
    c. clever
    d. hardworking

4. Our school rules do not <u>tolerate</u> any teasing.

   a. allow
   b. pursue
   c. mention
   d. punish

5. The governor tried to <u>conceal</u> his anger at the heckler.

   a. show
   b. hide
   c. demonstrate
   d. write

6. The incessant humming in his ears was quite <u>annoying</u>.

   a. bothersome
   b. loud
   c. unending
   d. controlling

7. Christopher Columbus was a bold, <u>adventurous</u> explorer.

   a. unusual
   b. precise
   c. daring
   d. outrageous

8. My sister <u>scoured</u> the house looking for her lost keys.

   a. cleaned
   b. wiped
   c. messed
   d. searched

9. We have had <u>compulsory</u> education in this country for generations.

   a. voluntary
   b. required
   c. free
   d. private

10. The sound of the car's horn is <u>peculiar</u> and high pitched.

   a. odd
   b. flawed
   c. weak
   d. strong

11. The <u>vast</u> expanse of the prairie stretches across several states.

    a. dry
    b. protected
    c. grassy
    d. immense

12. The vase was so <u>fragile</u> that I was hesitant to touch it.

    a. frosty
    b. expensive
    c. delicate
    d. light

13. Her energy was <u>surpassed</u> only by her desire to succeed.

    a. drained
    b. exceeded
    c. decreased
    d. equaled

14. After he was bitten by the neighbor's dog, he became very <u>timid</u> around all pets.

    a. angry
    b. fearful
    c. controlled
    d. disrespectful

15. I <u>despise</u> when I hear people calling other people unkind names.

    a. detest
    b. determine
    c. discriminate
    d. deserve

16. My teacher has such <u>diverse</u> interests that her reading list is very long.

    a. unusual
    b. common
    c. varied
    d. fine

17. Our computer lab assistant is quite <u>competent</u>.

    a. confused
    b. coordinated
    c. critical
    d. capable

Practice Skill: READING VOCABULARY - ANTONYMS

Expectation: Identify words with opposite meanings.

> Tip: An antonym is a word that means the opposite or nearly the opposite of another word (happy – sad). As you do the following exercises, read the sentence and focus on the underlined word by analyzing its precise meaning. Ask yourself: How is the word used in the sentence? What kind of a picture does it bring to mind? What are some synonyms for the underlined word? Then think of a word that can be used in the same context that conveys the opposite meaning. The goal is to find a word that negates as many attributes of the underlined word as possible.

Select the word that means the opposite of the underlined word.

Example: Even as a child, Steven enjoyed being <u>busy</u>.

> a. occupied
> b. bored
> c. lazy
> d. idle

The correct answer is *d*. Choice *a* is incorrect because *occupied* is a synonym for *busy*, not an antonym. Choices *b*, *c*, and *d* are possibilities that are related in meaning, but choices *b* and *c* imply an element of character that is not present in choice *d*. A person who is lazy or bored could still be busy, but a person cannot be busy and idle at the same time. The best answer is *d*. The words *idle* and *busy* are matter-of-fact terms that, at their core, concern an amount of activity.

1. She made an <u>inadvertent</u> comment that made us laugh.

> a. unintentional
> b. intentional
> c. enthusiastic
> d. amusing

2. After the drought, healthy plants were <u>sparse</u> on the range.

> a. dying
> b. frequent
> c. dry
> d. plentiful

3. Despite all of his awards, the general was a <u>humble</u> man.

    a. practical
    b. quiet
    c. conceited
    d. angry

4. We <u>encouraged</u> him to finish the project before the weekend.

    a. argued with
    b. troubled
    c. prevented
    d. pursued

5. The lawyers <u>accepted</u> their clients' desires to settle the lawsuit.

    a. surrounded
    b. forgot
    c. rejected
    d. understood

6. We had to <u>restrain</u> the horse in his stall.

    a. free
    b. try
    c. keep
    d. treat

7. My sister approached the stray cat <u>cautiously</u>.

    a. carefully
    b. carelessly
    c. courteously
    d. purposely

8. The teacher had a <u>private</u> talk with the principal.

    a. secret
    b. public
    c. crowded
    d. intelligent

9. Jaime did a very <u>thorough</u> job on the group project.

   a. complete
   b. effortless
   c. thoughtful
   d. incomplete

10. My father has a <u>logical</u> way of solving problems.

    a. thoughtful
    b. practical
    c. rational
    d. irrational

11. They made plans to move their offices to Florida on a <u>permanent</u> basis.

    a. temporary
    b. frequent
    c. infrequent
    d. proven

12. Most parents require their children to keep their rooms <u>tidy</u>.

    a. clean
    b. messy
    c. uncluttered
    d. dusted

13. The stretching exercises keep our muscles <u>flexible</u>.

    a. supple
    b. warm
    c. stiff
    d. strong

14. The color of the antique vase was quite <u>unique</u>.

    a. common
    b. unusual
    c. ugly
    d. old

15. The magicians made the tigers <u>vanish</u> in front of our eyes.

    a. erase
    b. appear
    c. growl
    d. attack

Practice Skill: VOCABULARY DEVELOPMENT - CONTEXT CLUES

Expectation: Use context clues to determine word meanings.

> Tip: When you come to an unfamiliar word in your reading there are strategies you can use to determine the word's meaning. One of the best strategies is to look at the way the word is used in the sentence. The meaning of the words you already know gives you clues about the meaning of the unknown word. This is called using context clues. The exercises in this section will give you practice in using this strategy.

EXERCISE # 1 – Read each sentence. Use context clues to determine the meaning of the underlined word. Choose the best answer.

Example: The government <u>confiscated</u> the money and property of the traitors.

    a. added to
    b. seized
    c. surprised
    d. borrowed

The correct answer is *b*. The government has special powers, and it would be likely to use them against traitors. This would make the other choices less logical than *b*.

1. The politician will lose votes if he does not change his <u>arrogant</u> attitude.

    a. kind
    b. self-important
    c. meek
    d. honest

2. The prospectors found <u>trace</u> amounts of gold in the stream, but no nuggets.

    a. huge
    b. very small
    c. wet
    d. bright

3. We will wait for the storm to <u>abate</u> before we leave to visit Grandma.

    a. rise
    b. dry
    c. increase in intensity
    d. decrease in intensity

4. Once baseball season starts, attendance at each game is <u>mandatory</u> for the players.

    a. voluntary
    b. sensible
    c. required
    d. possible

5. The bank robbers were unable to <u>evade</u> the police's search.

    a. recruit
    b. picture
    c. escape
    d. assist

6. The basketball team was forced to <u>forfeit</u> the game because their bus arrived after the start time.

    a. lose
    b. win
    c. analyze
    d. add

7. Although most of the cast members were nervous, Marta was <u>nonchalant</u> because she knew her lines for the play.

    a. proud
    b. concerned
    c. negative
    d. unconcerned

8. The low grade on the final exam caused Joe much <u>distress</u>.

    a. sorrow
    b. discovery
    c. difference
    d. support

9. Through hard work and constant effort, the farmer became one of the most <u>prosperous</u> members of the community.

    a. active
    b. wealthy
    c. unsuccessful
    d. caring

EXERCISE # 2 - Read the selection. Use context clues to select the best word to fill in a blank or to find a synonym for an underlined word.

Between 1848 and 1850, thousands of people from *[1]* <u>diverse</u> backgrounds came to California from all over the world. Although many of the forty-niners were men traveling __*[2]*___, a *[3]* <u>considerable</u> number of families also made the ___*[4]*__. Usually, gold fever was the *[5]* <u>impetus</u> for the trip, but even those who would not *[6]* <u>prospect</u> for gold hoped to *[7]* <u>establish</u> a better life and achieve *[8]* <u>prosperity</u> when they reached their *[9]* _____. The journey was an ___*[10]*__ sufficient to challenge even the bravest and heartiest __*[11]*__. For generations, Americans have paid *[12]* <u>tribute</u> to the *[13]* <u>indomitable</u> spirit and courage of the pioneers who settled California and the West.

1. a. different
   b. identical
   c. rich
   d. troubled

2. a. lazily
   b. unnecessarily
   c. alone
   d. certainly

3. a. suffering
   b. silent
   c. rather large
   d. endangered

4. a. journey
   b. book
   c. trade
   d. danger

5. a. motivation
   b. result
   c. transportation
   d. travel

6. a. build
   b. dream
   c. work
   d. search

7. a. watch
   b. destroy
   c. create
   d. troubleshoot

8. a. trouble
   b. success
   c. business
   d. conservation

9. a. provisions
   b. meeting
   c. concluded
   d. destinations

10. a. ordeal
    b. afterthought
    c. occupation
    d. ceremony

11. a. shipbuilders
    b. adventurers
    c. promises
    d. cooks

12. a. money
    b. respect
    c. disrespect
    d. passage

13. a. unworthy
    b. cowardly
    c. unconquerable
    d. destructive

Practice Skill: VOCABULARY DEVELOPMENT - MULTIPLE MEANINGS

Expectations: Identify words that have the same meaning. Recognize words with multiple meanings.

> Tip: Many words in the English language have more than one meaning. They can mean different things in different contexts. For example, the word "case" can refer to a case of soda, a case of measles, a legal case, or a briefcase. As you do the following exercises, think about the way the word is used in the particular phrase or sentence.

EXERCISE # 1 - Choose the best answer that fits both sentences.

Example:

The sun cast a bright _____.
The canoe was very _____.

     a. shine
     b. ray
     c. light
     d. tight

The correct answer is *c*. The best strategy is to substitute each of the possible choices in the blanks. Even if a word makes sense in one sentence (The sun cast a bright *ray*.), it may not make sense in the other (The canoe was very *ray*.). In the example, the word *light* makes sense in both sentences.

1. If I am the _____ one in the car, I close the door.
    How long is the storm expected to _____.

     a. winner
     b. first
     c. only
     d. last

2. The _____ signal indicated that the telephone was occupied.
    It might be dangerous to cross such a _____ street.

     a. flashing
     b. clean
     c. busy
     d. famous

3. The water caused a _____ in the circuit.
   Until my brother entered high school, he was _____ for his age.

   a. long
   b. short
   c. pool
   d. trial

4. The rental company charged a _____ rate of $20 per day for the car.
   The choir did not sing a _____ note all evening.

   a. sour
   b. flat
   c. musical
   d. cheap

5. My uncle is a very _____ and responsible person.
   The horse ran past the corral toward the _____ .

   a. stable
   b. strong
   c. lake
   d. smart

6. Shannon will never _____ of reading mysteries.
   I'm sure we have a spare _____ in the trunk of the car.

   a. dream
   b. change
   c. tire
   d. talk

7. The _____ of directors decided to sell the company.
   As soon as he gets a job, he will pay room and _____ to his parents.

   a. team
   b. movie
   c. representative
   d. board

8. The president's _____ set forth his goals for the next year.
   I will mail the package to your home _____.

   a. address
   b. talk
   c. speech
   d. present

EXERCISE # 2 ñ Read the sentences carefully. Select the sentence in which the underlined word has the same meaning as it has in the original sentence.

Example: We have a dinner <u>reservation</u> for 7:00 p.m.

    a. My only reservation about going on the trip was that I would miss school.
    b. I accepted the award without reservation.
    c. Our hotel reservation was for March 26.
    d. Our stay at the Navajo reservation was intriguing.

The correct answer is *c*. In both sentences, the word *reservation* refers to an advance arrangement.

1. She puts sunscreen on her <u>face</u> every morning.

    a. Saving face is important to their family and their culture.
    b. He tried to face his fears head on.
    c. We designed our garden to face north.
    d. His eyes were the most interesting part of his face.

2. The professor was a very <u>smart</u> dresser.

    a. My grandma always warns, ì Donít get smart with me, young lady.î
    b. The cut will smart for a little while.
    c. People who are smart often study every night.
    d. She wore a smart hat to the tennis match.

3. The judge will <u>order</u> the witnesses to tell the truth.

    a. The secretaryís job was to keep the desk, office, and files in good order.
    b. The shoe store will order a pair of shoes in your size if you need them.
    c. Our assignment was to put the words in alphabetical order.
    d. When a general gives an order, the soldiers will obey.

4. Every day my grandma eats <u>part</u> of an apple.

    a. The actress plans to audition for a part in the play.
    b. If you travel to more than one part of the country, it will take several days.
    c. The barber usually likes to part his hair on the side.
    d. Friends never part in anger.

5. A block of granite is a <u>solid</u> material.

    a. When ice melts it is no longer in the solid state.
    b. Mr. Solis is known to be a solid citizen.
    c. We waited three solid hours for the plane to arrive.
    d. There is solid support in the legislature for the pending bill.

Practice Skill: SENTENCE STRUCTURE AND WORD USAGE

Expectation: Use correct sentence structure and parts of speech.

Tip: The skills that you will practice in this section will help you to develop a clear, effective writing style. Although this may sound like a tall order, the task is not as difficult as it sounds. Once the content of a piece of writing is fully developed and all the thoughts you want to express appear on the paper, it is time to turn your rough draft into a final, polished piece of writing. To do this, analyze each sentence by asking two questions: Does the sentence clearly express a complete thought? Does the sentence fit in with the rest of the sentences?

EXERCISE # 1 – Read each sentence. For each one, determine whether it is a complete sentence, a sentence fragment, a comma splice, or a run-on sentence. Select the best answer from the following choices:

   a. **complete sentence**
   b. **sentence fragment**
   c. **comma splice**
   d. **run-on or rambling sentence**

Example: I love my dog, I love my cat.

The correct answer is *c*. The writer has made a comma splice error by combining two simple sentences with a comma. (The comma should be replaced by a semicolon or a period.)

1. Thinks he's a real comedian.

2. Go today?

3. After school, he went to the store, the bike shop, and the post office.

4. Mom treated us to a frozen yogurt then we went to the library to get a book for my report on penguins and Antarctica for social studies, my favorite class which usually is science, depending on how good the teacher is.

5. I have always wanted to travel far enough north to see a herd of caribou graze freely and grizzly bears catch fish in the icy rivers to share with their cubs.

6. If ever I could do it.

7. You could read the book, you could see the movie, too.

EXERCISE # 2 – Select the word that best completes the sentence.

1. We _____ advantage of the low prices to buy some new shoes yesterday.

    a. takes
    b. taked
    c. took
    d. take

2. The funniest part of the book _____ when the twins are mistaken for each other.

    a. were
    b. been
    c. are
    d. is

3. Javier _____ his bicycle to the park to practice special stunts.

    a. will bringed
    b. bringed
    c. brought
    d. bringing

4. Tanya and Tarryn _____ so much time together that they are starting to talk alike.

    a. are spending
    b. is spending
    c. was spending
    d. had spended

5. That's not the way we _____ to prepare our voices before a concert.

    a. suppose
    b. supposed
    c. were suppose
    d. are supposed

6. I never _____ walked to the corner without my jacket in such cold temperatures.

    a. woulda
    b. would of
    c. would have
    d. would

EXERCISE # 3 – Read each sentence to find one that is grammatically correct.

1. a. He insisted on completing the homework assignment all by hisself.
    b. *The Borrowers* are a great book.
    c. My favorite kind of orange contains no seeds.
    d. How many chairs need to be setted around the table?

2. a. Jimmy did not feel well when he woke up today.
    b. Jimmy did not feel good when he woke up today.
    c. It is not a well idea to stay up late before a test.
    d. The velvet feels very well when I touch it.

3. a. I never knew how many books he bought at the book swap.
    b. I never knew how many books he bringed to the book swap.
    c. I never seen so many books as they had at the book swap this year.
    d. All are correct.

4. a. The customers waited patient and calm for their turn in line.
    b. The clerk behind the counter worked quick.
    c. The food that he left outside freezed harder than an iceberg.
    d. None are correct.

5. a. The first book in the series is funner to read than the second one.
    b. She combed her hair in an effort to look more pretty.
    c. None berries are ripe this time of year.
    d. None are correct.

6. a. We had began to race before we heard the starting buzzer.
    b. After we beginned the test, we had to stop for a fire drill.
    c. The key to writing a gooder short story is to make people laugh.
    d. None are correct.

7. a. I digged through the wastebasket to find my missing homework.
    b. My aunt must have went away because she has not answered her phone all week.
    c. You have been working so hard, you might as well take a break.
    d. None are correct.

8. a. I think you could be a little more careful when you cross the street.
    b. I think you could be a little carefuller when you cook on the stove.
    c. Haven't you heard that we winned the game?
    d. We won the game after Terrance catched the fly ball.

Practice Skill: FIGURATIVE LANGUAGE

Expectation: Recognize the use of figurative language.

Tip: Good writers use figurative language to bring a vivid picture to the reader's mind. A figure of speech is not to be taken literally, but it can be used instead of an adjective or adverb to bring color and life to writing. A simile is a figure of speech that uses "as" or "like" to make a comparison. (The drill sergeant was as tough as granite.) A metaphor is a figure of speech that directly compares two things without using the words "like" or "as." (I enjoy talking to Poindexter, the walking dictionary.) Personification is a special type of metaphor in which a non-human thing such as an idea, an object, or an animal is given human qualities. (The tree branch reached out to grab the child running through the dense forest.)

Read each sentence to see if it contains figurative language. Select the best answer from the following choices:

        a. metaphor
        b. simile
        c. personification
        d. no figurative language

1. She bit the beef jerky like a puppy with a chew toy.

2. The clouds wept on the sidewalk as the pedestrians scurried on the sidewalk.

3. Her hair looked like a dish mop.

4. The fish were jumping in the lake like popcorn kernels in a microwave.

5. The thunder bellowed its mighty roar to announce the arrival of the storm.

6. My grandpa's first car was a rusty bucket of bolts with a seat and a spare tire.

7. She grinned the widest smile I had ever seen.

8. The clouds were pillows in the blue blanket sky.

9. The blimp looked like a beluga whale surfing through waves of clouds.

10. As much as I am enjoying this song, I must turn off the radio and do my homework.

Practice Skill: CAPITALIZATION AND PUNCTUATION

Expectation: Use correct capitalization and punctuation.

Tip: If you doubt the importance of using correct punctuation and capitalization in your writing, try reading this: once the content of a piece of writing is fully developed a writer must pay close attention to the conventions of standard english the grammar punctuation and capitalization in order to turn a rough draft into a final polished piece of writing capitalization and punctuation serve as signals or clues to help the reader decipher meaning they are as important to your writing as stop signals and green and yellow lights are to pedestrians and drivers so do your readers a favor show them some respect by using correct punctuation and capitalization

EXERCISE # 1 – CAPITALIZATION
In each of the following exercises, decide whether the text is without capitalization errors, or whether it should be revised according to one of the choices.

Example:

Mrs. Smith and steven went to a museum.

a. Mrs Smith and steven went to a museum.
b. Mrs. Smith and Steven went to a museum.
c. Mrs. Smith. and Steven went to a Museum.
d. No errors

The correct answer is *b*. The first letter in the sentence and the proper nouns are capitalized, but the common noun is not.

1. Shannon attends the fourth grade in Mrs. Johnson's class at Poway School.

a. Shannon attends the Fourth Grade in Mrs. Johnson's Class at Poway School.
b. Shannon attends the fourth Grade in Mrs. Johnson's class at Poway school.
c. Shannon attends the fourth grade in Mrs. Johnson's class at poway school.
d. No errors

2. It is easy to see mt. whitney from lone pine, California.

a. It is easy to see Mt. whitney from Lone pine, California.
b. It is easy to see mt. whitney from Lone Pine, California.
c. It is easy to see Mt. Whitney from Lone Pine, California.
d. No mistakes

3. The Portland trailblazers are my favorite players in the national basketball association.

    a. The Portland trailblazers are my favorite players in the National basketball association.

    b. The Portland Trailblazers are my favorite players in the National Basketball Association.

    c. The Portland Trailblazers are my favorite players in the national basketball association.

    d. No errors

4. On the second monday in february, school will be closed for presidents' day.

    a. On the Second Monday in February, School will be closed for Presidents' Day.

    b. On the second monday in February, school will be closed for Presidents' day.

    c. On the second Monday in February, school will be closed for Presidents' Day.

    d. No errors

5. "But, Dad," protested Jason, "If I clean the garage, I. won't have time to play ball."

    a. "But, dad," Protested Jason, "if I clean the garage, I won't have time to play ball."

    b. "But dad," protested jason, "if I clean the garage, I won't have time to play ball."

    c. "But, Dad," protested Jason, "if I clean the garage, I won't have time to play ball."

    d. No errors

6. If you ever get the chance, be sure to read *the adventures of Tom Sawyer*.

    a. If you ever get the chance, be sure to read *The Adventures of Tom Sawyer*.

    b. If You ever get the chance, be sure to read *The Adventures Of Tom Sawyer*.

    c. If you ever get the chance, be sure to read *The Adventures Of Tom Sawyer*.

    d. No errors

7. If I could speak French as it is spoken in France, I could work at the United Nations or at the Eiffel Tower.

    a. If I could speak french as it is spoken in france, I could work at the united nations or at the eiffel tower.

    b. If I could speak french as it is spoken in France, I could work at the united nations or at the eiffel tower.

    c. If I could speak french as it is spoken in France, I could work at the United Nations or at the Eiffel Tower.

    d. No errors

8. If I could journey back in time, I would want to visit the Middle Ages and either be the King of England or a knight on a Lipizzaner stallion.

    a. If I could journey back in time, I would want to visit the middle ages and either be the King of England or a knight on a lipizzaner stallion.
    b. If I could journey back in time, I would want to visit the middle ages and either be the King of England or a Knight on a Lipizzaner stallion.
    c. If I could journey back in time, I would want to visit the Middle Ages and either be the king of England or a knight on a lipizzaner stallion.
    d. No errors

9. President Bush's Father was also a president of our nation.

    a. President Bush's father was also a President of our nation.
    b. President Bush's father was also a president of our nation.
    c. President Bush's father was also a President of our Nation.
    d. No errors

10. After my Mom came in the room, we called Aunt Mo at Dad's request.

    a. After my mom came in the room, we called aunt mo at dad's request.
    b. After my Mom came in the room, we called aunt Mo at Dad's request.
    c. After my mom came in the room, we called Aunt Mo at Dad's request.
    d. No errors

11. Have you ever watched "Once upon a time in the Wild West" on KCET?

    a. Have you ever watched "Once upon a time in the wild West" on Kcet?
    b. Have you ever watched "Once Upon a Time in the Wild West" on KCET?
    c. Have you ever watched "Once Upon A Time In The Wild West" on KCET?
    d. No errors

12. Congress and the national security Council oversee the CIA.

    a. Congress and the national security council oversee the CIA
    b. Congress and the National security council oversee the Cia.
    c. Congress and the National Security Council oversee the CIA.
    d. No errors

13. Argentina is a country located on the continent of South America.

    a. Argentina is a Country located on the Continent of South America.
    b. Argentina is a country located on the continent of south america.
    c. Argentina is a country located on the continent of south America.
    d. No errors

EXERCISE # 2 – PUNCTUATION

In each of the following exercises, decide whether the text is without punctuation errors, or whether it should be revised according to one of the choices.

Example:

When did Mrs Smith, Karla, and Steven climb Mt Whitney.

  a. When did Mrs Smith Karla and Steven climb Mt. Whitney?
  b. When did Mrs. Smith, Karla, and Steven climb Mt. Whitney?
  c. When did Mrs. Smith, Karla, and Steven, climb Mt. Whitney?
  d. No errors

The correct answer is *b*. The missing periods after *Mrs.* and *Mt.*, and the question mark missing in the original sentence appear in choice *b*. Choice *a* is not punctuated correctly because it is missing commas to separate the words in a series (*Mrs. Smith, Karla, and Steven*). Choice *c* is not correct because it contains an extra comma after *Steven*.

1. "Can I march in the parade, Dad asked Julie?".

  a. "Can I march in the parade, Dad? asked Julie."
  b. "Can I march in the parade, Dad?" asked Julie.
  c. "Can I march in the parade, Dad," asked Julie.
  d. No errors

2. "Strike three! You're out!" yelled the umpire.

  a. "Strike three, you're out?" yelled the umpire!
  b. Strike three. You're out, yelled the umpire.
  c. "Strike three! You're out! yelled the umpire."
  d. No errors

3. The farmer, grew corn, beans, lettuce, and tomatoes, every year.

  a. The farmer grew, corn, beans, lettuce, and tomatoes, every year.
  b. The farmer grew corn; beans; lettuce; and tomatoes every year.
  c. The farmer grew corn, beans, lettuce, and tomatoes every year.
  d. No errors

4. In the astronomers opinion, the comet will not be visible to Nashville Tennessee until June, 24, 2020

  a. In the astronomer's opinion the comet will not be visible to Nashville Tennessee until June 24, 2020.
  b. In the astronomer's opinion, the comet will not be visible to Nashville, Tennessee, until June, 24, 2020.
  c. In the astronomer's opinion, the comet will not be visible to Nashville, Tennessee until June 24, 2020.
  d. No errors

5. Were going to go fishing, hiking, boating, and swimming, on vacation.

   a. Were going to go fishing, hiking, boating, and swimming on vacation.
   b. We're going to go fishing, hiking, boating, and swimming on vacation.
   c. We're going to go, fishing, hiking, boating, and swimming, on vacation.
   d. No errors

6. "Come here Buttercup" said the farmer to his cow.

   a. "Come here, Buttercup," said the farmer to his cow.
   b. "Come here Buttercup, said the farmer to his cow."
   c. "Come here, Buttercup." said the farmer to his cow.
   d. No errors

7. Lets give the dog its bone or it will growl at us.

   a. Let's give the dog it's bone or it will growl at us.
   b. Let's give the dog its bone or it will growl at us.
   c. Let's give the dog its' bone or it will growl at us.
   d. No errors

8. Jans sister didnt' understand her science teachers instructions'.

   a. Jan's sister didnt understand her science teachers instructions.
   b. Jan's sister didn't understand her science teachers' instructions'.
   c. Jan's sister didn't understand her science teacher's instructions.
   d. No errors

9. I asked Jeans sister what she wants to be when she grows up?

   a. I asked Jean's sister what she wants to be when she grows up.
   b. I asked Jean's sister what she want's to be when she grows' up.
   c. I asked Jean's sister what she wants to be when she grows up?
   d. No errors

10. Mark Twain's <u>Tom Sawyer</u> is one of my favorite children's books.

   a. Mark Twains <u>Tom Sawyer</u> is one of my favorite childrens books.
   b. Mark Twain's <u>Tom Sawyer</u> is one of my favorite childrens' books.
   c. Mark Twains' <u>Tom Sawyer</u> is one of my favorite childrens' books.
   d. No errors

Practice Skill: SPELLING

Expectation: Identify words that are spelled correctly and incorrectly.

Tip: Keep a list of any words that you frequently misspell. When you add a word to the list, carefully print the word correctly. Touch each letter as you spell the word out loud. Visualize the letters in your mind. Keep the list handy as you write and refer to it as you proofread your writing. The more you are aware of your spelling habits, the faster your spelling will improve.

EXERCISE # 1 - Identify the word that is spelled incorrectly:

1. a. above   b. adresses   c. although   d. afterward

2. a. agriculture   b. access   c. accurit   d. attitude

3. a. apiece   b. appreciate   c. advencher   d. attention

4. a. approximately   b. apolagize   c. boundary   d. brief

5. a. believe   b. brought   c. business   d. becuase

6. a. bottum   b. caution   c. casual   d. choose

7. a. choice   b. cercumstances   c. completely   d. courage

8. a. describe   b. desireable   c. design   d. dictionary

9. a. doubt   b. dollar   c. dilishus   d. drawn

10. a. embariss   b. emphasize   c. equator   d. electric

11. a. enthusiastic   b. espeshally   c. environment   d. explain

12. a. field   b. incurage   c. fault   d. favorite

13. a. fasinating   b. foreign   c. fragile   d. friendship

14. a. genuine   b. gilty   c. government   d. gentle

15. a. guess   b. governer   c. history   d. gradually

16.	a. happen	b. height	c. hansome	d. handled
17.	a. hesitate	b. hospital	c. happenning	d. height
18.	a. insted	b. imaginary	c. important	d. immediate
19.	a. improvement	b. impossable	c. individual	d. illegal
20.	a. irragate	b. jury	c. justice	d. judge
21.	a. jelous	b. journey	c. judgment	d. jewelry
22.	a. knickels	b. knew	c. knight	d. knot
23.	a. key	b. knowlege	c. kindness	d. kingdom
24.	a. laid	b. languich	c. laughter	d. legendary
25.	a. lenkth	b. likable	c. lessons	d. liar
26.	a. legislature	b. liquid	c. lonely	d. lonelyness
27.	a. mission	b. mashine	c. misunderstand	d. muddy
28.	a. mountain	b. months	c. mistery	d. multiply
29.	a. neither	b. nieghbor	c. neglect	d. nurse
30.	a. never	b. naturly	c. niece	d. none
31.	a. niether	b. occasion	c. necessary	d. only
32.	a. often	b. official	c. obay	d. oxygen
33.	a. paragraph	b. paralel	c. particular	d. peaceful
34.	a. persuade	b. peice	c. photograph	d. pleasant
35.	a. probally	b. quickest	c. quarter	d. precious
36.	a. question	b. qualm	c. quiat	d. quite
37.	a. realize	b. raise	c. request	d. reconize
38.	a. reasonable	b. responsabilaty	c. regular	d. received

EXERCISE # 2 – Fill in the blank with the word that is spelled correctly for the context.

1. If you _____ milk at the store, be sure to get your change.

   a. by
   b. bye
   c. buy
   d. biy

2. We _____ a message in a bottle to see how far it would travel.

   a. cent
   b. sent
   c. scent
   d. sendt

3. I am not sure _____ movie they are going to see.

   a. which
   b. witch
   c. wich
   d. whitch

4. I hope _____ time to eat lunch.

   a. its
   b. it's
   c. its'
   d. its's

5. Tara is younger _____ her brother.

   a. thin
   b. then
   c. thun
   d. than

6. We do not always have to be _____ in the library.

   a. quite
   b. quit
   c. quiet
   d. quiat

7. The catcher _____ the ball to third base.

    a. threugh
    b. through
    c. thorough
    d. threw

8. To develop your ability to express yourself, _____ in a journal every day.

    a. rite
    b. right
    c. write
    d. wright

9. _____ do you want to go after school today?

    a. Where
    b. Were
    c. Wear
    d. Ware

10. John and Jackson want _____ lunches from the kitchen.

    a. there
    b. their
    c. they're
    d. thier

11. Kobe was wondering when _____ going to win the playoffs.

    a. there
    b. their
    c. they're
    d. thier

12. Do you know _____ ball is rolling down the street?

    a. who's
    b. whos'
    c. whose'
    d. whose

13. I am just _____ tired for a walk right now.

    a. to
    b. too
    c. two
    d. toe

Practice Skill: ROOTS AND AFFIXES

Expectation: Use knowledge of word origins and word parts to determine word meanings.

> Tip: In addition to using context clues to determine the meaning of unfamiliar words, roots and affixes also give clues to word meanings. Greek and Latin roots (think of them as word families) make up more than half of all words in the English language. Affixes, called prefixes when they are at the front of a word and suffixes when they end a word, also give clues about a word's meaning. If you learn to recognize certain roots and affixes, you can make educated guesses about word definitions. The exercises in this section will give you practice in using these strategies.

Examples:

Common prefixes and their meanings:
- re – means to "do again" or "from"
- un – means "not"
- equa – means "like" or "same"
- dis – means "not"
- de – means "separate"
- mis – means "not" or "wrongly"
- pre – means "before"

Common suffixes and their meanings:
- -er – one who does
- -ful – full of
- -able – able to
- -ship – the condition of
- -ly – in the manner of
- -tion – the state of
- -less – without

Latin word roots:
- spec – means "look" or "sec"
- segregare – means to "separate"
- script – means "to write"
- port – means "to carry"
- dict – means "say"
- mot – means "move"

Greek word roots:
- arch – "ruler"
- grapho – "write, draw"
- poly – "many"
- therm – "heat"
- onym – "name"
- chrono – "time"

Select the word that best matches the given meaning:

1. Able to be understood

   a. understanding
   b. laughable
   c. adorable
   d. understandable

2. condition of starving

    a. foodition
    b. eatless
    c. starvation
    d. none of the above

3. without worth

    a. worthless
    b. cash
    c. value
    d. priceless

4. not honest

    a. honorarium
    b. honorees
    c. dishonest
    d. none of the above

5. determined ahead of time

    a. undetermined
    b. indeterminable
    c. determination
    d. predetermined

6. not necessary

    a. necessarily
    b. unnecessary
    c. necessity
    d. none of the above

7. full of suspense

    a. suspenseful
    b. suspension
    c. suspended
    d. none of the above

8. not able to be beaten

    a. beatable
    b. unbeatable
    c. beaten
    d. beater

9. polysyllabic

   a. ugly sided
   b. made of aluminum
   c. having many syllables
   d. none of the above

10. dictation

   a. saying something out loud for someone else to write
   b. silent movie making
   c. mental picture
   d. roadside station

11. transcript

   a. written copy
   b. purpose
   c. bridge
   d. carry

12. loving music

   a. musical
   b. harmonica
   c. philharmonic
   d. chromatic

13. electricity produced by heat

   a. thermostat
   b. thermometer
   c. thermonuclear
   d. thermoelectricity

14. partly solid

   a. hemisphere
   b. semisolid
   c. solidified
   d. solution

Practice Skill: READING COMPREHENSION

Expectation: Understand a variety of grade-level-appropriate materials.

> Tip: Good readers think about what they are reading. When they read something new, they make predictions about what they will read and what they may learn. They look at pictures, titles, and key words to get an overview. Then, as they read, they make a mental note of whether their predictions are confirmed. Another important skill that they practice is restating what they read all along the way.

EXERCISE # 1 - Read the selection and select the best answer to the questions that follow:

The Forty-Niners

[A]   Between 1848 and 1850, thousands of people from diverse backgrounds came to California from all over the world. The greatest migration occurred in 1849, when 80,000 people traveled to California, either by land or by sea. Although many of them were men traveling alone, a considerable number of families also made the journey. Usually a bad case of gold fever motivated the trip, but even those who would not search for gold hoped to make a better life and prosper when they reached California.

[B]   In the month April of 1849 alone, about 30,000 people set out for California by land. The forty-niners crammed food, tools, and whatever worldly possessions they could fit into their wagons. The journey was grueling and not for the faint of heart. Those who traveled west via an overland route often faced blistering sun, harsh winds, walnut-sized hailstones, and numbing snowfall, all in the same trip. By the time the travelers reached the Rocky Mountains, they were looking for ways to speed up the journey and lighten the load for their oxen or horses about to begin the treacherous climb. At the approach to the Rocky Mountains, the trail was littered with every item imaginable, from chests of drawers to cast-iron stoves. In addition to the difficulties imposed by the severe elements and the geographic challenges, the travelers faced hunger, thirst, illness, and the threat of attacks from Indians who were afraid that the settlers would take their homelands. Of all of the perils, the latter was the one the forty-niners encountered least often.

[C]   Despite the hardships presented by land travel, many forty-niners preferred the overland route to the two sea route alternatives. These were not luxury cruises! The trip from New York to California by ship required an 18,000 mile voyage around the tip of South America. Sea travelers faced months of storms, seasickness, stale water, and spoiled food in cramped, unsafe ships. Another faster way to reach California still required a 12,000 mile ocean voyage. This route involved taking one ship to Panama, then crossing Panama by mule

and canoe, and finally boarding another ship to travel the rest of the way to San Francisco. An added danger on this route was the exposure to deadly tropical diseases (cholera and malaria) in Panama. On another route, the forty-niners sailed down the Atlantic Coast, around Florida, and across the Gulf of Mexico to Texas. From Texas, they walked 4,000 miles across Mexico's deserts to the California gold fields.

[D]   No matter the route, it was no easy journey. But in 1849, a trip to California was the only known cure for gold fever! People's desires to rid themselves of the symptoms and break the fever helped to propel California into statehood in 1850.

1. In section [A], the word *migration* means

    a. moving from one place to settle in another.
    b. traveling down river on a steamship, canoe, or paddleboat.
    c. leading a revolution against the government.
    d. none of the above

2. According to the selection, people with a bad case of gold fever

    a. got sick and died.
    b. decided not to make the trip to California.
    c. were not allowed into California.
    d. decided to travel to California.

3. A forty-niner who traveled 2,200 miles to California must have traveled which route?

    a. by sea around Cape Horn
    b. by sea to Panama, and by sea again to California
    c. by land across the prairies and Rocky Mountains
    d. across Texas and Mexico

4. Why did the forty-niners throw their belongings aside along the way?

    a. There were no laws against littering.
    b. They wanted other travelers to buy them.
    c. They wore them out early in the trip.
    d. It would be easier for the oxen or horses to pull the wagons up the steep mountains.

5. What were the elements referenced in section [B]?

    a. the weight of the loaded wagons
    b. the sun, wind, hail, and snow
    c. the mountains and rivers that slowed progress to California
    d. hunger, thirst, illness, and Indian attacks

6. What is the main idea of section [B]?

    a. Sea travelers faced many difficult challenges.
    b. A trip to California cured gold fever.
    c. Overland travelers faced many difficult challenges.
    d. The Rocky Mountains were a geographic challenge faced by forty-niners traveling by land.

7. What detail supports the main idea of section [B]?

    a. Sea travelers faced months of storms, seasickness, stale water, and spoiled food in cramped, unsafe ships.
    b. The greatest migration occurred in 1849 when 80,000 people traveled to California either by land or by sea.
    c. In addition to the difficulties imposed by the severe elements and the geographic challenges, the pioneers faced hunger, thirst, illness, and the threat of attacks from Indians who were afraid that the settlers would take their homelands.
    d. At the approach to the Rocky Mountains, the trail was littered with every item imaginable, from chests of drawers to cast-iron stoves.

8. What is the main idea of section [C]?

    a. Sea travelers faced many difficult challenges.
    b. A trip to California cured gold fever.
    c. Overland travelers faced many difficult challenges.
    d. The Rocky Mountains were a geographic challenge faced by forty-niners traveling by land.

9. What detail supports the main idea of section [C]?

    a. Sea travelers faced months of storms, seasickness, stale water, and spoiled food in cramped, unsafe ships.
    b. The greatest migration occurred in 1849 when 80,000 people traveled to California either by land or by sea.
    c. In addition to the difficulties imposed by the severe elements and the geographic challenges, the pioneers faced hunger, thirst, illness, and the threat of attacks from Indians who were afraid that the settlers would take their homelands.
    d. At the approach to the Rocky Mountains, the trail was littered with every item imaginable, from chests of drawers to cast-iron stoves.

10. An example of the author's opinion is

    a. In the month of April of 1849 alone, about 30,000 people set out for California by land.
    b. The journey was grueling and not for the faint of heart.
    c. Another faster way to reach California still required a 12,000 mile ocean voyage.
    d. All of the above

11. Which of the following details is irrelevant to this selection?

    a. California's constitution did not allow slavery within the state.
    b. Once the forty-niners arrived in California, it was difficult to send or receive mail.
    c. The California missions had been established before the Gold Rush.
    d. All of the above

12. After reading in section [B] that overland travel "was grueling and not for the faint of heart," a reader might make one of the following predictions. Which of the predictions is confirmed by the selection?

    a. Land travelers would face difficulties and dangers including bad weather, hunger, thirst, and illness.
    b. Indian attacks were the primary danger of overland travel.
    c. The Rocky Mountains posed no special problems to land travelers.
    d. The weather and geography posed no major challenges to land travelers.

13. What is the most likely cause for land travelers approaching the Rocky Mountains to want to "speed up the journey?"

    a. They wanted to get to California before all the gold was gone.
    b. They wanted to see the view from the summit and claim the land for America.
    c. Their oxen and horses were building stamina and could cover more ground in a day.
    d. They wanted to cross the mountains before snow started falling.

14. What was a principal effect of gold fever on our nation's history?

    a. More people studied medicine to find a cure for such diseases.
    b. More people learned about the exotic animals of Panama.
    c. The population of California grew large enough to qualify for statehood.
    d. The price of gold became the topic of conversation all over the world.

Complete the chart below based on the "Forty-Niners" selection.

_____[15]_____

LAND
    2,200 miles from Missouri to California,
    by mule or ____[16]____ pulled by oxen or horses

SEA
    18,000 miles from New York to California,
    down ____[17]____ Coast around South America to California

LAND and SEA
    ____[18]____ mile sea voyage in two separate parts,
    across Panama by mule and canoe, then north to California
        OR
    down Atlantic Coast around ____[19]____ and through Gulf of Mexico,
    overland 4,000 miles through ____[20]____ to California

---

15. a. Routes to California in 1849
    b. Land Routes to California in 1849
    c. Sea Routes to California in 1849
    d. Gold Fever and the Forty-Niners

16. a. steamship
    b. wagon
    c. freight train
    d. clipper ship

17. a. Atlantic
    b. Pacific
    c. Gulf
    d. Mississippi

18. a. 18,000
    b. 12,000
    c. 2,200
    d. 4,000

19. a. Panama
    b. Cape Horn
    c. Florida
    d. Baja California

20. a. Panama
    b. Isthmus of Panama
    c. Missouri River
    d. Texas and Mexico

EXERCISE # 2 – Read the selection and select the best answer to the questions that follow.

Have You Seen the Elephant?

Many forty-niners used axle grease to print slogans on their wagons, such as "Rough and Ready," "Westward Ho" and "California or Bust." Many of the slogans appear on modern day bumper stickers and still speak clearly to us today. However, the most popular slogan seen on wagons in 1849 referred in some way to "seeing the elephant." That is one slogan that Americans are unlikely to see on car bumpers in the twenty-first century.

"Have You Seen the Elephant?" was a question frequently posed on the overland trails in 1849. Forty-niners said good bye to their friends and loved ones by announcing that they were "going to see the elephant." Newspaper cartoons of 1849 showed miners panning for gold next to an elephant. Forty-niners who made it to California wrote home to say they had "seen the elephant from the tip of his trunk to the end of his tail." Those who abandoned the trek and returned home said that they had seen the "elephant's tracks."

Of course, "seeing the elephant" was a figure of speech not to be taken literally. What was the source of this expression and what did it mean? Long before the gold rush, there was a popular story about when elephants began leading circus parades from place to place in America. According to the tale, a farmer wanted to see the circus that was coming to town, and he loaded his wagon full of vegetables to sell once he reached the town. On the way, he encountered the circus parade with an elephant in front. The man was overjoyed, but his horse was frightened. The horse bolted, the cart overturned, and the vegetables were lost. But the farmer was unfazed. "I don't care," commented the farmer, "for I have seen the elephant."

Based on that story, "seeing the elephant" came to mean overcoming hardships to face the adventure of a lifetime. The tale perfectly paralleled the experience of the forty-niners who traveled by land or sea as part of the California gold rush. It was exciting and dangerous all the way.

1. What is the main idea of the selection?

    a. Circus elephants can be frightening to animals.
    b. Facing your fears can be dangerous to the food supply.
    c. Farmers are brave, curious, and adventurous.
    d. "Seeing the elephant" came to mean coming to California during the gold rush.

2. What is a slogan?

    a. a motto, or a phrase that advertises a purpose
    b. a daring adventure
    c. a modern invention
    d. the adventure of a lifetime

3. When the writer says that "seeing the elephant" was a figure of speech not to be taken literally, what does she mean?

   a. Elephants were extinct in the United States in the nineteenth century.
   b. Many forty-niners wanted to see a circus elephant on the road to California.
   c. The elephant symbolized the adventures that the forty-niners encountered.
   d. Many forty-niners reported seeing elephants on their trips to California.

4. What happened to those who "saw the elephant tracks"?

   a. They fell on the trail and were trampled by the elephants.
   b. They joined the circus.
   c. They decided not to go all the way to California.
   d. They followed the tracks all the way to California.

5. Someone who had "seen the elephant from the tip of his trunk to the end of his tail" probably

   a. saw the circus on the way to California.
   b. had a tough time on the road to California and in the gold fields, too.
   c. was just leaving home for California.
   d. had an uneventful trip to California.

6. Why was the farmer *unfazed* in the story?

   a. He didn't eat vegetables, so he didn't care that they spilled.
   b. He was not upset because he really didn't want to see the circus anyway.
   c. He was quite upset that his vegetables were ruined.
   d. He was not upset about losing the vegetables because seeing the elephant was so exciting.

7. What does it mean to say that the "tale perfectly paralleled the experience of the forty-niners"?

   a. The tail of the elephant looked like the trail that the travelers followed.
   b. The elephant led the circus parade and the forty-niners blazed the trail to California.
   c. The forty-niners faced danger and excitement on the way to the gold fields, just like the farmer faced the excitement and danger on the way to see the circus.
   d. The hardships faced by the forty-niners on the road to California were not worth the gold or the adventure.

8. An example of the author's opinion in this selection is:

   a. The tale perfectly paralleled the experience of the forty-niners.
   b. "I don't care," commented the farmer, "for I have seen the elephant."
   c. Many forty-niners used axle grease to print slogans on their wagons.
   d. Newspaper cartoons of 1849 showed miners panning for gold next to an elephant.

EXERCISE # 3 – Read the selection and select the best answer to the questions that follow.

The Nature of Happiness
A Look at Leo Tolstoy's "The Two Brothers"

You may have heard the old adage "Beauty is in the eye of the beholder." In his short story, "The Two Brothers," Leo Tolstoy raises the same issue with respect to happiness. What is happiness? What would you risk to have happiness in your life? These are questions that you will think about as you read Tolstoy's profound story.

In the story, two brothers discover a stone with writing on it. The writing instructs the reader to travel into the forest, swim across a river, steal bear cubs from a mother bear, and run away with them up a mountain without looking back. At the summit, the writing predicts that the reader will see a house in which the reader will find happiness.

The younger brother is eager to begin the adventure, but the older brother is against the idea for several reasons. He doubts that the writing is true and thinks it may be a joke. Even if it could be true, he worries that they might get lost in the forest, drown crossing the river, or get eaten by the mother bear. Additionally, the older brother wonders aloud about the kind of happiness that might be found at the house. He warns his brother to take care not to overlook the small pleasures in life while seeking greater happiness, and he reminds him that a bird in the hand is worth two in the bush.

The arguments of the older brother fail to dissuade the younger sibling. In the view of the younger brother, the mere fact that they found the rock was reason enough to trust in its truth. He sees no harm in trying to find happiness. Why should they leave the stone for someone else to find the happiness that they desire and deserve? In his view, nothing of great value comes easily, and it is only through hard work that one can achieve success. Finally, he says that he does not want anyone to consider him to have been afraid to take the chance.

The younger brother sets off on the journey, leaving his older brother behind. He ventures into the forest, finds and swims across the river, steals the cubs of a sleeping mother bear, and runs up the mountain without looking back. When he reaches the mountain top, people greet him, take him to their city, and crown him their king. After reigning for years, another king wages war against him, conquers the city, and drives him out.

The younger brother returns home, where the brothers have a joyous reunion and recount the events that have occurred since their paths diverged. The older brother insists that he made the right decision. Although he has grown neither rich nor poor, he has consistently been living quietly and well. He contrasts his lot with the troubles that his brother has endured during his reign as king. But the younger brother maintains that he has no regrets. Although he has nothing now, he is pleased that he will always have something to remember, something in his view that his brother is lacking.

1. This selection summarizes a story that is about:

   a. what happiness means to different people.
   b. the dangers of wandering through the forest.
   c. two brothers who disagree about war.
   d. two brothers who do not like each other.

2. An adage is

   a. a wise man.
   b. a well-known saying or proverb.
   c. a mysterious poem.
   d. a way to fix what ails you.

3. As it is used to describe "The Two Brothers," the word "profound" means

   a. wandering.
   b. disturbing.
   c. obvious on its face.
   d. going deeper than what is clear on the surface.

4. Which brother would be most likely to agree with Mark Twain's comment, "Twenty years from now you will be more disappointed by the things that you didn't do than by the ones you did do."

   a. the older brother
   b. the younger brother
   c. neither brother
   d. both brothers

5. What saying in the selection expresses the view that having something is better than risking having nothing?

   a. A rolling stone gathers no moss.
   b. He who laughs first laughs last.
   c. A bird in the hand is worth two in the bush.
   d. He who is afraid of the leaves must not go into the forest.

6. What does it mean to say that "the arguments of the older brother failed to dissuade the younger sibling"?

   a. The older brother could not convince the younger brother that he should not go into the forest.
   b. The older brother convinced the younger brother that he should not go into the forest.
   c. The older brother was talking to the stone.
   d. The brothers did not try to change each other's minds.

EXERCISE # 4 – Read the selection and answer the questions that follow.

Operating Instructions: Zontron Model SB 246 Cordless Telephone

Installation
- Plug the charger into an electrical outlet.
- Charge the battery for the cordless telephone by placing the telephone on the charger. The battery must charge for a full 8 hours before the phone is operable. When the battery is low and in need of a charge, the red light on the telephone will flash. After the initial charge, the average charge time is 3-4 hours.

Making Calls
- Press TALK button. Dial the party's telephone number.
- To hang up, press TALK again or place the telephone on the charger.

Answering Calls
- Press TALK. If the telephone is on the charger, just lift it off the charger and speak into the telephone.
- If the telephone rings 5 times, the internal answering machine will answer the call and record any message left by the caller.

Listening to Messages
- When the green light flashes on the MAIL button, there is an unheard message. Press MAIL to listen to the message. To erase the message, press DELETE. To save the message, press SAVE. The yellow light will flash on the MAIL button.

---

1. What must be done in order to make the phone operable?

   a. Press the TALK button.
   b. Record a message greeting.
   c. Plug in the charger and place the telephone on the charger for 8 hours.
   d. All of the above

2. In order to end a phone call, what must be done?

   a. Press talk.
   b. Place the telephone on the charger.
   c. All of the above
   d. None of the above

3. What does a flashing yellow light on the telephone mean?

   a. The battery is low and needs recharging.
   b. There is an unheard message waiting.
   c. There is a message waiting that has been heard and saved.
   d. A message has been deleted.

4. What happens when the telephone rings 5 times?

   a. The call is lost.
   b. The call is automatically answered and a message is recorded.
   c. The yellow light flashes.
   d. The battery will charge automatically.

ANSWER KEY
LANGUAGE ARTS

Synonyms
1. A
2. B
3. C
4. A
5. B
6. A
7. C
8. D
9. B
10. A
11. D
12. C
13. B
14. B
15. A
16. C
17. D

Antonyms
1. B
2. D
3. C
4. C
5. C
6. A
7. B
8. B
9. D
10. D
11. A
12. B
13. C
14. A
15. B

Context
Exercise 1
1. B
2. B
3. D
4. C
5. C
6. A
7. D

8. A
9. B

Context
Exercise 2
1. A
2. C
3. C
4. A
5. A
6. D
7. C
8. B
9. D
10. A
11. B
12. B
13. C

Multiple Meanings
Exercise 1
1. D
2. C
3. B
4. B
5. A
6. C
7. D
8. A

Exercise 2
1. D
2. D
3. D
4. B
5. A

Sentence Structure
Exercise 1
1. B
2. B
3. A
4. D
5. A
6. B

7. C

Exercise 2
1. C
2. D
3. C
4. A
5. D
6. C

Exercise 3
1. C
2. A
3. A
4. D
5. D
6. D
7. C
8. A

Figurative Language
1. B
2. C
3. B
4. B
5. C
6. A
7. D
8. A
9. B
10. D

Capitalization/ Punctuation
Exercise 1
1. D
2. C
3. B
4. C
5. C
6. A
7. D
8. D
9. B
10. C
11. B
12. C
13. D

ANSWER KEY
LANGUAGE ARTS

Capitalization/
Punctuation
Exercise 2
1. B
2. D
3. C
4. C
5. B
6. A
7. B
8. C
9. A
10. D
Spelling
1. B
2. C
3. C
4. B
5. D
6. A
7. B
8. B
9. C
10. A
11. B
12. B
13. A
14. B
15. B
16. C
17. C
18. A
19. B
20. A
21. A
22. A
23. B
24. B
25. A
26. D
27. B
28. C
29. B

30. B
31. A
32. C
33. B
34. B
35. A
36. C
37. D
38. B
Spelling
Exercise 2
1. C
2. B
3. A
4. B
5. D
6. C
7. D
8. C
9. A
10. B
11. C
12. D
13. B
Roots and
Affixes
1. D
2. C
3. A
4. C
5. D
6. B
7. A
8. B
9. C
10. A
11. A
12. C
13. D
14. B

Reading
Comprehension
1. A
2. D
3. C
4. D
5. B
6. C
7. C
8. A
9. A
10. B
11. D
12. A
13. D
14. C
15. A
16. B
17. A
18. B
19. C
20. D
Exercise 2
1. D
2. A
3. C
4. C
5. B
6. D
7. C
8. A
Exercise 3
1. A
2. B
3. D
4. B
5. C
6. A
Exercise 4
1. C
2. C
3. C
4. B

NOTES

MATH

Practice Skill: WHOLE NUMBER CONCEPTS AND COMPUTATION

Expectations: Add, subtract, multiply, and divide with accuracy.

Tip: By the end of grade four, students are expected to understand whole numbers in the millions and to master the steps to accurately add, subtract, multiply, and divide multidigit numbers. In order to accomplish this, it is essential to have automatic recall of the basic facts in all four operations. Also, practice the following skills to make whole number math a snap:

    1. Practice some mental math every day. Try to add a two-digit number and a one-digit number in your head. (34 + 7 = 41). Then try multiplying a two-digit number by a one-digit number. See if you can carry in your head. (42 x 6 = 252).

    2. Practice math strategies such as doubling (15 x 2 = 30, 36 x 2 =72) estimating (99 x 4 = approximately 100 x 4 = 400), and multiplying numbers by 10, 100, and 1,000 (65 x 10 = 650, 65 x 100 = 6,500, 65 x 1,000 = 65,000).

    3. When working problems on paper, be as neat as you can be. Keep each problem in its own space and line up columns and digits as if you were working on graph paper. Take special care to recopy problems correctly. (If neatness is a challenge for you, try actually working problems on graph paper to help keep straight columns.)

Choose the best answer. Example:

    A hot air balloon can lift 700 pounds. Steve weighs 110 pounds, Alex weighs 140 pounds, Manuel weighs 95 pounds, and Billy weighs 176 pounds. What is the boys' combined weight?

    a. 531 pounds
    b. 521 pounds
    c. 221 pounds
    d. not here

The correct answer is "b". Add the boys' weights to find the total. The weight that the balloon can lift is unnecessary information in this problem. Estimate the answer to check whether your calculation makes sense and whether you can eliminate other choices as being unreasonable. (100 + 100 + 100 + 200 = 500 is an estimate that eliminates choice "c" and is close to the actual answer of 521.) It is necessary to solve the actual problem to its conclusion, however, in order to know for sure whether the answer is 521, 531, or another that is "not here" among the choices.

1. Find the difference between 63,726 and 28,008.

   a. 21,276
   b. 34,718
   c. 35,718
   d. not here

2. What is the sum of 47,303 and 29,467 ?

   a. 66,760
   b. 76,760
   c. 17,836
   d. not here

3. What is the product of 54 and 154 ?

   a. 208
   b. 100
   c. 8,316
   d. not here

4. Find the quotient if the divisor is 9 and the dividend is 7,785.

   a. 856
   b. 865
   c. 69,615
   d. not here

5. There were 3,465,254 golf balls manufactured each month at the San Diego Golf Ball Factory. The factory operates 5 days a week. If 1,000 of the golf balls are seconds that cannot be sold, how many balls can be sold each month?

   a. 3,654,254 golf balls
   b. 3,365,154 golf balls
   c. 2,465,254 golf balls
   d. 3,464,254 golf balls

6. In problem # 5 above, if the golf balls are sold with 3 balls in a box, <u>approximately</u> how many boxes of balls are boxed for sale each month?

   a. 150,000 golf balls
   b. 1,150,000 golf balls
   c. 15,000,000 golf balls
   d. not here

7. Tiger uses 12 buckets of balls practicing at the golf range every day. If the average bucket of balls contains 15 boxes of San Diego Golf Ball Factory golf balls, how many balls does Tiger hit in daily practice?

    a.   180 balls
    b.   540 balls
    c.   480 balls
    d.   not here

8. Which product is the greatest?

    a.   826 x 10
    b.   226 x 100
    c.   60 x 60
    d.   55 x 550

9. Which equation is true?

    a.   364 x 3 = 182 x 6
    b.   364 x 3 = 182 x 4
    c.   362 x 3 = 282 x 6
    d.   362 x 6 = 182 x 9

10. What property does the following number sentence show?

$$39 + 52 = 52 + 39$$

    a.   The property of zero for addition
    b.   The distributive property
    c.   The commutative property of addition
    d.   The associative property of addition

11. What property does the following number sentence show?

$$(3 + 9) + 12 = 3 + (9 + 12)$$

    a.   The property of zero for addition
    b.   The distributive property
    c.   The commutative property
    d.   The associative property of addition

12. What property does the following number sentence show?

$$46 \times 3 = (40 + 6) \times 3 = (40 \times 3) + (6 \times 3)$$

    a.   The property of zero for addition
    b.   The distributive property
    c.   The associative property of multiplication
    d.   The commutative property of multiplication

13.	700	14.	38,056	15.	7,928
	−227		−29,482		+ 2,464

a.	483	a.	8,574	a.	5,464
b.	573	b.	8,674	b.	10,302
c.	583	c.	9,874	c.	9,392
d.	473	d.	not here	d.	not here

16. Which of the following statements about multiplication is true?

    a. An example of the commutative property of multiplication is 16 x 2 = 2 x 16.

    b. An example of the associative property of multiplication is
          (3x 25) x 4 = 3 x (25 x 4).

    c. An example of the property of one for multiplication is 8 x 1 = 8.

    d. All of the above

17. Which of the following statements is <u>not</u> true?

        a. a > b means a is greater than b.

        b. n < 7 means n is less than 7.

        c. (13 + 7) + 6 > 13 + (7 + 6).

        d. If 14 x n = 0, then n = 0.

18.	8,794	19.	62,854	20.	6,007
	x 7		x 12		x 28

a.	57,558	a.	632,248	a.	12, 196
b.	59,558	b.	62,866	b.	168,196
c.	61,558	c.	744,248	c.	48,056
d.	not here	d.	not here	d.	not here

21.	2)498	22.	4)724	23.	6)24024

a.	299	a.	18 R 1	a.	4004
b.	234	b.	181	b.	404
c.	239	c.	171	c.	6006
d.	not here	d.	not here	d.	not here

24.	5)20,020	25.	7)3,980	26.	7)789

a.	4,040	a.	568	a.	172
b.	404	b.	568 R 4	b.	1,721
c.	4,004	c.	600	c.	112 R 5
d.	not here	d.	not here	d.	not here

27. $10\overline{)2,070}$

 a. 2,070
 b. 27
 c. 270
 d. not here

28. $34\overline{)9,724}$

 a. 286
 b. 285 R 34
 c. 301
 d. not here

29. $27\overline{)1,566}$

 a. 580
 b. 58
 c. 75
 d. not here

30. $20\overline{)2,070}$

 a. 27
 b. 13 R 5
 c. 103
 d. not here

31. $25\overline{)750}$

 a. 3
 b. 34
 c. 30
 d. not here

32. $72\overline{)40,608}$

 a. 564
 b. 58 R 8
 c. 5,064
 d. not here

33. $1,286 \div 24$

 a. 643
 b. 53
 c. 53 R 14
 d. not here

34. $5,008 \div 42$

 a. 119
 b. 119 R 10
 c. 11 R 38
 d. not here

35. $6086 \div 34$

 a. 20 R 9
 b. 17 R 30
 c. 179
 d. not here

36. $\begin{array}{r} 78 \\ \times\ 5 \\ \hline \end{array}$

 a. 840
 b. 390
 c. 354
 d. not here

37. $\begin{array}{r} 66 \\ \times 39 \\ \hline \end{array}$

 a. 792
 b. 2,574
 c. 1,800
 d. not here

38. $\begin{array}{r} 4007 \\ \times\ \ 48 \\ \hline \end{array}$

 a. 192,336
 b. 19,536
 c. 16,056
 d. not here

Practice Skill: NUMBER SENSE AND NUMERATION

Expectations: Understand place value from hundredths to millions and the
relationships among numbers of various magnitudes.
Understand how whole numbers and decimals relate to simple
fractions.
Use concepts of negative numbers.
Know how to factor small whole numbers.

Tips: When a number is written in digits, it is written in **standard form** (5,978). A number is written in **expanded form** when it is written as the sum of the value of its digits (5000 + 900 + 70 + 8). A place value chart from hundredths to millions can be useful to help you remember the value of digits in numbers.

Parts of a set or a whole can be expressed as **decimals** or **fractions**. In the number 6.57, the decimal point separates the whole number 6 from the decimal 57 hundredths. As a fraction, the same number can be expressed as $6\frac{57}{100}$.

Positive numbers are all numbers that are greater than 0, while **negative** numbers are less than 0. When measuring temperature in cold climates, negative numbers are frequently used. (-5°F).

To find the **factors** of a number, identify the numbers that divide exactly into that number. For example, the factors of 16 are 1, 2, 4, 8, and 16. A **prime number** is a positive whole number whose only factors are itself and 1. (7 is a prime number because it is evenly divisible only by 1 and 7. Contrast that with 15, whose factors are 1, 3, 5, and 15).

Choose the best answer.

1. Which number is written correctly?

   a. 786,07.02
   b. 80,08.10
   c. 8874,038
   d. 4,568,980

2. Which number is represented by (7 x 1,000,000) + (6 x 10,000) + (3 x 1,000) + (5 x 100) + (4 x 10) + (9 x 1)?

    a. 763,549
    b. 7,643,549
    c. 7,060,549
    d. 7,063,549

3. Which number has the digit 9 in the hundred thousands place?

    a. 6,905,432
    b. 6,090,432
    c. 6,300,932
    d. 9,609,432

4. Which of the following shows the standard form of nine million, four hundred three thousand, thirty-eight and sixty-two hundredths?

    a. 9,043, 386.02
    b. 9,000,000) + 400,000 + 3,000 + 30 + 8 + 0.60 + 0.02
    c. 9,403,038.62
    d. 9,430,380.62

5. Round 8,729,041 to the nearest hundred thousand.

    a. 8,729,000
    b. 9,000,000
    c. 8,700,000
    d. 8,730,000

6. Which value is the greatest?

    a. 4013.16
    b. 4013.06
    c. 4052.06
    d. 4052.26

7. Which answer is ordered from least to greatest?

    a. 41.02, 4,110.2, 4,102.11
    b. 311.02, 301.02, 302.01
    c. 64.03, 310.30, 2,103.03
    d. 723.4, 702.34, 7,234.12

8. Which statement is <u>not</u> true?

    a. 78 < 89
    b. 0.01 > 0.1
    c. −7 > −10
    d. 114.22 > 114.12

9. Which statement is <u>not</u> true?

    a. $\dfrac{1}{2} = 0.5$

    b. $\dfrac{1}{2} = .50$

    c. $\dfrac{7}{4} = 1\dfrac{1}{4}$

    d. $\dfrac{7}{4} = 1.75$

10. Which temperature is the coldest?

    a. −6°F
    b. 0°F
    c. −1°F
    d. 0.5°F

11. Which of the following is <u>not</u> a prime number?

    a. 7
    b. 27
    c. 13
    d. 17

12. What are all the factors of 36?

    a. 1, 36
    b. 1, 2, 18, 36
    c. 1, 2, 3, 4, 5, 9, 10, 11, 36
    d. 1, 2, 3, 4, 6, 9, 12, 18, 36

Practice Skill: MEASUREMENT AND GEOMETRY

Expectation: Understand plane and solid geometric shapes and use this knowledge to show relationships and solve problems. Understand various metric units of measure.

Tip: Memorize the following formulas for **polygons**:
Perimeter (distance around the edge)→add the lengths of the sides;
Area (square units) of a rectangle → Area = length x width (A =lw)
    The area is always expressed in square units.
Volume (area inside) of a rectangular solid →
      Volume = area of the base of the prism x height (V = Bh), or
           length x width x height (V = lwh) Express volume in cubic units.
A **circle** is not a polygon. Its perimeter is called the **circumference**. The **diameter** divides a circle into 2 **congruent** parts. The **radius** of a circle is ½ the length of the diameter. →
    Memorize the **metric** units of measure and know their relative sizes:
    The basic metric unit of length is a **meter** (approximately 3 feet long). There are 100 **centimeters** in a meter and 1,000 **millimeters** in one meter. (100 cm=1 m and 1,000 mm=1 m). While a millimeter is a very small unit, a **kilometer** is used to measure long distances. It takes 1,000 meters to make a kilometer.
    The basic metric unit of measure for capacity is a **liter**. There are 1,000 **milliliters** in one liter.
    The basic metric unit of measure for weighing mass is a **gram**. There are 1,000 grams in a **kilogram**.
    The basic metric unit for measuring temperature is a **degree Celsius**. Water freezes at 0° Celsius and boils at 100° Celsius.

Example: What is the area for the shaded space inside the figure below?

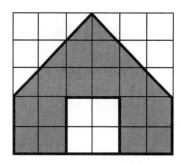

   a. 24 units^2
   b. 17 units^2
   c. 20 units^2
   d. 19 units^2

The correct answer is ì bî. To get this, you count the total number of shaded squares (14). Then count the shaded triangles (6). Two triangles equal one square unit. So, 14 + 3 = 17

Choose the best answer. If the correct answer is not one of the choices, select the choice ì not here.î

1. Which of these triangles are congruent?

     Fig. 1   Fig. 2   Fig. 3   Fig. 4

   a. Figures 1, 2, 3, and 4
   b. Figures 2 and 3
   c. Figures 1 and 4
   d. not here

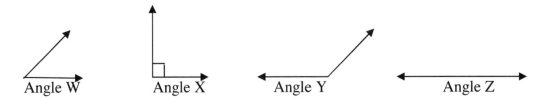

Angle W   Angle X   Angle Y   Angle Z

2. Which angle is an obtuse angle with a measurement of greater than 90°?

   a. Angles W and X
   b. Angles W and Z
   c. Angles X, Y and Z
   d. not here

3. Which angle measures 90° ?

   a. Angle W
   b. Angle X
   c. Angle Y
   d. Angle Z

4. Which figure has perpendicular lines?

   a. Angle W
   b. Angle Z
   c. Angle X
   d. not here

5. Which pair of lines is parallel?

Fig. A   Fig. B   Fig. C

   a. Figures A and C
   b. Figure A
   c. Figure B
   d. Figure C

6. Which line segment is a diameter of this circle?

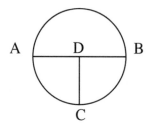

   A   D   B

           C

   a. $\overline{AB}$

   b. $\overline{AC}$

   c. $\overline{AD}$

   d. $\overline{CD}$

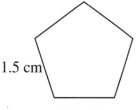

1.5 cm

Fig. G

1.75 cm

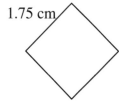

Fig. H

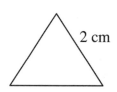

2 cm

Fig. I

7. Which of the following is a true statement about Figures G, H, and I?

   a. The perimeter of Figure G is 7.5 cm.
   b. The perimeter of Figure G is 7.5 cm^2.
   c. The area of figure H is 7 cm^2.
   d. The perimeter of Figure G is equal to the perimeter of Figure I.

8. Which of the following is a true statement?

   a. 60 cm = 600 mm
   b. 3000 km = 3 m
   c. An elephant's weight would usually be measured in milliliters.
   d. A hummingbird's weight would usually be measured in kilograms.

9. Which of the following is a true statement?

   a. Degrees Celsius have no equivalent in degrees Fahrenheit.
   b. Water boils at 0° C.
   c. Water freezes at -10° C.
   d. -2° C is warmer than -10° C.

10. What are the coordinates of the end points of the line segment?

   a. (0,4) (0, -4)
   b. (6,2) (-4,-8)
   c. (2,6) (-8,-4)
   d. not here

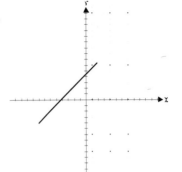

11. What is the diameter of a circle with a radius of 24 cm?

   a. 12 cm
   b. 48 cm
   c. 8 cm
   d. not here

12. How many faces does a cube have?

   a. 3
   b. 12
   c. 6
   d. not here

For exercises 13 – 16, fill in the blanks by referring to Figures W, X, Y, and Z. Select the best answer from the following choices:

   a. scalene triangle
   b. equilateral triangle
   c. isosceles triangle
   d. right triangle

          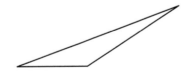

Figure W   Figure X   Figure Y   Figure Z

Figure W is a(n) ____13____. Figure X is a(n) ____14____. Figure Y is a(n) ____15____.

Figure Z is a(n) ____15____.

Practice Skill: STATISTICS AND PROBABILITY

Expectation: Interpret numerical data and make predictions for simple probability situations.

Tip: To solve problems involving statistical data, arrange the set of data in order from least to greatest before performing any calculations.

Range – the difference between the least and the greatest number in the set.

Mean or Average – the sum of all the data divided by the number of addends.

Median – the middle in a set of data that is arranged in order of value. If there is no "middle" number, average the two numbers in the middle of the data set to find the median.

Mode – the number that appears most often in a set of data. (There can be more than 1 mode.)

Outlier – a number in the set of data that is much greater or less than the other items in the set of data.

For example, working with the data set of quiz scores 10, 10, 8, 5, 7, 9, 10, 5

Reorder the data → 5, 5, 7, 8, 9, 10, 10, 10

Range →10 – 5 = 5

Mean →(5 + 5 +7 + 8 + 9 + 10 + 10 + 10) ÷ 8 = 8

Median → (8 + 9) ÷ 2 = 8 $\frac{1}{2}$

Mode →10

To express the probability or chance that an event will occur, describe the situation verbally (3 out of 4) or numerically in a fraction (3/4). The denominator of the fraction represents the total outcome, while the numerator represents the favorable outcome or results wanted. For example: There are 7 marbles in a bag; 2 of them are blue and the rest are white. The probability of reaching into the bag without looking and pulling out a red marble is 0/7 (impossible) because there are no red marbles in the bag. The probability of pulling out a blue marble is 2/7 or 2 out of 7. The probability of pulling out a white marble is 5/7 or 5 out of 7. It is more likely then, that a white marble will be taken from the bag than a blue one.

Use the following information to answer exercises 1 - 4. Select the best answer.

Every Friday, Mr. Gonzales gives a 10-question quiz in his math class. Serena's scores for the first six weeks of school were 8, 10, 6, 5, 9, 10.

1. What was Serena's mean score on the quizzes at the end of the first six weeks?

    a. 10
    b. 8
    c. 5
    d. 8.5

2. What was the range of Serena's scores?

    a. 10
    b. 8
    c. 5
    d. 8.5

3. What was the median score?

    a. 8
    b. 5
    c. 8.5
    d. 10

4. What is the mode of Serena's scores?

    a. 8
    b. 5
    c. 8.5
    d. 10

Use the following tree diagram to answer questions 5 - 7.

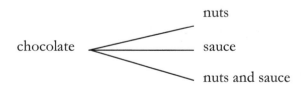

5. This tree diagram could be used to predict the possible outcomes of which of the following fact patterns?

    a. At the ice cream shop, the menu lists 4 flavors of ice cream and 2 toppings. How often are chocolate sundaes sold at the ice cream shop?

    b. The menu at the cafe lists 2 ice cream choices and 6 different toppings. How many different sundaes does the cafe offer?

    c. The menu at the PTA after-school picnic offered pizza and salad, and a choice of ice cream sundaes or cookies for dessert. How much ice cream should the PTA buy?

    d. not here

6. How many different kinds of single scoop sundaes are there to choose from?

    a. 2
    b. 4
    c. 6
    d. not here

7. If strawberry ice cream is also offered, how many different kinds of single scoop sundaes will it be possible to make?

    a. 3
    b. 6
    c. 9
    d. not here

Exercises 8 - 9 refer to the following fact pattern:

Tammy has 3 pairs of white socks, 2 pairs of cream socks, 1 pair of socks with her initials embroidered on them, and 1 pair of tall soccer socks. She rolls each pair of socks into a ball to keep them separate. Every morning, Tammy plays a guessing game. She reaches into the drawer without looking and predicts which pair of socks she will grab.

8. On Monday, Tammy guesses that she will grab a pair of white socks. What are the chances that Tammy will pick a pair of white socks?

    a. 2/7
    b. 3/7
    c. 1/4
    d. 3/4

9. The chances are the same that Tammy will choose:

    a. purple or white
    b. white or cream
    c. initialed socks or soccer socks
    d. all of the above

Practice Skill: FRACTIONS AND DECIMALS

Expectation: Understand different interpretations of fractions: that fractions may represent parts of a whole, parts of a set, and division of a whole number by a whole number. Understand equivalent fractions. Understand how whole numbers and decimals relate to simple fractions. Add and subtract simple fractions and decimals.

Tip: For fractions, practice doubling patterns such as halves, quarters, eighths, and sixteenths. Visualize odd numbered denominators by picturing a loaf of bread. (Five slices of a loaf of bread cut into 13 slices is 5/13 of the loaf.) Think of decimals as fractions with denominators of 10 or 100. Money shows decimal relationships. Because there are 100 cents in 1 dollar, a penny is .01 (one hundredth) of 1 dollar. A dime is 10/100 or .10 of a dollar. Ten hundredths can be reduced to its simplest form: 1/10 or .1 .

Choose the best answer.

Use the diagram to answer questions 1 and 2.

1. Look inside the large rectangle. What fraction of the shapes are circles?

    a. 3/12
    b. 4/4
    c. 1/5
    d. 1/3

2. What fraction of the shapes are polygons?

    a. 4/12
    b. 12/12
    c. 8/12
    d. 1/3

3. A large pizza has 16 slices. 3/4 of the pizza has been eaten. How many slices have been eaten?

    a. 4 slices
    b. 12 slices
    c. 6 slices
    d. 8 slices

4. Which of the following numbers are common multiples of 3 and 4?

    a. 3, 4, 7, 11, 16
    b. 12, 24, 36, 48
    c. 3, 4, 6, 8, 9, 12
    d. 1, 3, 2, 4

5. Which fractions are listed in simplest form from least to greatest?

    a. $\dfrac{6}{12}, \dfrac{2}{12}, \dfrac{7}{12}, \dfrac{12}{12}$

    b. $\dfrac{2}{12}, \dfrac{6}{12}, \dfrac{7}{12}, \dfrac{12}{12}$

    c. $\dfrac{6}{12}, \dfrac{1}{2}, \dfrac{2}{24}, \dfrac{1}{12}$

    d. $\dfrac{1}{12}, \dfrac{1}{4}, \dfrac{1}{2}, \dfrac{7}{12}$

6. Which number represents 2 whole cookies and 3 out of 5 pieces of another cookie?

    a. $2\dfrac{5}{3}$ b. $\dfrac{5}{5}$ c. $2\dfrac{3}{5}$ d. $\dfrac{5}{2}$

7. Which decimal has the same value as $^\circ$?

    a. .14
    b. .41
    c. .75
    d. .25

8. Which decimal has the same value as $\dfrac{275}{100}$?

    a. .275
    b. 1.75
    c. 27.5
    d. 2.75

9. $\dfrac{2}{7} + \dfrac{3}{7} =$

   a. $\dfrac{5}{7}$ b. $\dfrac{5}{14}$ c. $\dfrac{2}{7}$ d. $\dfrac{1}{7}$

10. $\dfrac{5}{12} + \dfrac{1}{6} =$

   a. $\dfrac{2}{12}$ b. $\dfrac{7}{12}$ c. $\dfrac{6}{18}$ d. $\dfrac{1}{3}$

11. $3\dfrac{1}{5} + 2\dfrac{2}{5} =$

   a. $\dfrac{8}{5}$ b. $5\dfrac{3}{10}$ c. $5\dfrac{3}{5}$ d. $\dfrac{8}{10}$

12. $\dfrac{7}{12} \ \tilde{n} \ \dfrac{5}{12} =$

   a. $\dfrac{7}{12}$ b. 2 c. $\dfrac{2}{0}$ d. $\dfrac{1}{6}$

13. $\dfrac{3}{8} \ \tilde{n} \ \dfrac{1}{16} =$

   a. $\dfrac{5}{16}$ b. $\dfrac{2}{16}$ c. $\dfrac{2}{8}$ d. $\dfrac{2}{12}$

14. $\dfrac{3}{10}$

  $\tilde{n} \ \dfrac{1}{5}$

  _____

   a. $\dfrac{2}{10}$ b. $\dfrac{2}{5}$ c. $\dfrac{1}{10}$ d. $\dfrac{1}{5}$

In exercises 15 - 23, compare the two numbers. Select and answer from the following:

                  a.   >
                  b.   <
                  c.   =

15.   ½ ◯ 0.75

16.   5.82 ◯ 5.79

17.   6.28 ◯ 6.4

18.   ¼ ◯ 0.25

19.   3.13 ◯ $3\dfrac{13}{100}$

20.   0.6 ◯ 0.06

21.   6.35 ◯ 4.89

22. $\dfrac{6}{10}$ ◯ 0.75

23. $\dfrac{6}{5}$ ◯ 1.5

24. $3.89 + 9.5 + 5 =$

    a.   18.39   b.   17.9   c.   12.9   d.   48.9

25. $5.5 - 3.48 =$

    a.   2   b.   2.12   c.   2.02   d.   1.02

26. $4.97 + 176.3 =$

    a. 176.397   b.   16.27   c.   18.127   d.   181.27

27. Round 3,759.79 to the nearest tenth.

    a. 3,759
    b. 3, 759.8
    c. 3,760
    d. not here

Practice Skill: PATTERNS AND RELATIONSHIPS

Expectation: Analyze patterns and relationships in order to predict the additional items in a series.

Tip: To find a missing number in a sequence, analyze the pattern by determining how each number is related to the next number. To check your answer, identify the mathematical equation within the pattern and then apply it to the entire series.

Example: Fill in the blank.

ABBC, BCCD, _____, DEEF

a. CBBD   b. CDDE   c. DCCE   d. EFFG

The correct answer is "b". The first letter in each item is in alphabetical order, followed by the doubling of the next alphabetical letter and ending with a single alphabetically ordered letter in the chain.

Choose the correct answer.

1. Which will come next?   25, 20, _____, 10, 5

     a. 10
     b. 15
     c. 30
     d. 25

2. Which rule is correct for the following?   3, 14, 36, 80,

     a. y x 2 + 2
     b. y + 4 x 2
     c. y + 3 x 3
     d. y + 2 x 2

3. Which pattern is next?

     a.   b.   c.   d.

4. Which fraction does not belong in the pattern?   1/3, 4/5, 3/9, 4/12

     a. 1/3   b. 4/5   c. 3/9   d. 4/12

Practice Skill: ESTIMATION

Expectation: Estimate sums, differences, products, and quotients.

> Tip: Most people use estimating skills every day in one way or another. Practice estimating the cost of groceries on your next trip to the market. Chances are that many adults in the market will be estimating the cost of their groceries, too! At school, use estimation to quickly check whether an answer to a math problem makes sense as a solution. In both situations, we estimate by rounding some numbers to those that are easy to work with. Another way of estimating is to use "compatible numbers" (numbers that are mentally easy to work with) to help calculate the exact answer to a problem. This is an effective way to simplify a math problem as you work it out. For example, $51\overline{)362}$ is about $50\overline{)350}$, so the first digit that you would try in the quotient is a 7, and the exact answer to the problem will be close to 7.

Example: Mrs. Smith bought 9 greeting cards at $ 1.95 each. About how much did they cost all together?

      a. $9.00   b. $19.99   c. $18.00   d. $25.00

The correct answer is "c". To determine "about" how much, use estimation skills. Round$1.95 to $2.00. (9 x $2.00 = $18.00)

1. Estimate the quotient for 569 ÷ 8 =

    a. 60
    b. 65
    c. 70
    d. 50

2. Estimate the product for 98 x 12 =

    a. 1200
    b. 9080
    c. 1400
    d. 140

3. About how much will it cost to buy 4 steaks priced at $3.96, $4.69, $5.24, and $4.83?

    a. $12.00   b. $14.00   c. $16.00   d. $19.00

4. About how much money should Monica plan to spend if she buys a dozen lilies at $3.95 each? Be sure to overestimate in case she is charged sales tax.

    a. $30.00   b. $35.00   c. $40.00   d. $50.00

Grade 4 Edition

76

Practice Skill: ALGEBRA AND FUNCTIONS

Expectations: Use variables, mathematical symbols, and properties to write
and simplify expressions and sentences. Know how to manipulate equations.

Tip: When you solve problems, you will need to know how to change verbal
phrases into algebraic expressions. For example, if you know that Sung is 7
years younger than fifteen-year-old Jaime, you can state this algebraically
by assigning letters to what you want to know and restating the
relationships. → S represents Sung, and J represents Jaime.
$$S = J - 7 \text{ (Sung's age is Jaime's age less 7 years)}$$
$$S = 15 - 7 \text{ (you know Jaime is 15, so substitute 15 for J)}$$
$$S = 8 \qquad \text{(compute and solve for S. Sung is 8 years old.)}$$
Check by substituting the answer in the original problem. "8-year-old Sung
is 7 years younger than 15-year-old Jaime. 8 = 15 – 7 and 8 is 7 less than 15.

**EXERCISE #1 - Rewrite the phrase or sentence in algebraic terms. Choose the best
answer.**

1.   10 less than a number

    a. $x - 10$
    b. $x + 10$
    c. $10 - x$
    d. $10x$

2.   8 more than a number

    a. $a - 8$
    b. $a + 8$
    c. $8a$
    d. $a \div 8$

3. the sum of 6 and n

    a. $6 - n$
    b. $n\text{-}6$
    c. $n + 6$
    d. $6n$

4. the product of a and 7

    a. $a + 7$
    b. $a - 7$
    c. $a \div 7$
    d. $7a$

5. a number increased by 10

    a. $y - 10$
    b. $10 - y$
    c. $10y$
    d. $y + 10$

6. a number decreased by 12

    a. $x - 12$
    b. $12 - x$
    c. $12x$
    d. $x + 12$

7. 13 decreased by a number n

    a. $n - 13$
    b. $13n$
    c. $13 - n$
    d. $13 + n$

8. half of a number

    a. $c \div 5$
    b. $c \div 2$ or ½ c
    c. $c - \frac{1}{2}$
    d. $c + \frac{1}{2}$

9. Four greater than x is fifteen.

    a. $x - 15 = 4$
    b. $x - 4 - 15$
    c. $x + 4 = 15$
    d. $15 + 4 = x$

10. Three less than y is twelve.

    a. $y - 3 = 12$
    b. $y + 3 = 12$
    c. $3y = 12$
    d. $y - 3 = 12$

11. Seventeen is the product of 2 and x.

    a. $17 = 2x$
    b. $17 = 2 \div x$
    c. $17 = 2 + x$
    d. $17 = x - 2$

12. Forty is one-half of y.

    a. $40 = 2y$
    b. $40 = 2 + y$
    c. $40 = y - 2$
    d. $40 = \frac{1}{2} y$

13. Four times c is one hundred.

    a. $c = 100$
    b. $4 + c = 100$
    c. $4c = 100$
    d. $c^4 = 100$

14. The product of 7 and z is 70.

    a. $7z = 70$
    b. $7 \div z = 70$
    c. $z - 7 = 70$
    d. $z + 7 = 70$

15. The sum of z and 8 is 12.

    a. $z + 12 = 8$
    b. $z + 8 = 12$
    c. $z - 8 = 12$
    d. $8z = 12$

16. q is the product of 15 and 4.

    a. $q = 15 - 4$
    b. $q = 15(4)$
    c. $q = 15 \div 4$
    d. none of the above

17. x decreased by 8 is 3.

    a. $x = x - 8$
    b. $x + 8 = 3$
    c. $x - 8 = 3$
    d. none of the above

18. y is 3 less than seventeen.

    a. $y = 3 - 17$
    b. $y = 3 + 17$
    c. $y = 3 \div 17$
    d. $y = 17 - 3$

19. The quotient when twelve is divided by m is four.

    a. $12 = 4 \div m$
    b. $12 - 4 = m$
    c. $4 = 12m$
    d. $4 = \dfrac{12}{m}$

20. The product of eleven and twelve is m.

    a. $11 \cdot 12 = m$
    b. $11 \div 12 = m$
    c. $11 + 12 = m$
    d. $11 - 12 = m$

EXERCISE # 2 - Complete each equation so it is balanced.

Example: $(2 + 5) + 8 = 6 + \square$

    a. 8
    b. 9
    c. 2
    d. 10

The correct answer is *b*. The left side of the equation totals 15. In order for the equation to be balanced, the right side of the equation must also total 15. Since 6 + 9 equals 15, the missing number to balance the left side is 9.

1. $3 + 4 + \square = 9 + 2$

    a. 7
    b. 11
    c. 4
    d. not here

2. $6 + 6 + 7 = \square + 5 + 3 + 2$

    a. 7
    b. 19
    c. 6
    d. not here

3. $\square + 13 + 5 = 18 + 7$

    a. 7
    b. 5
    c. 15
    d. not here

4. $9 + \square + 10 = 17 + 3$

    a. 3
    b. 1
    c. 17
    d. not here

5. $(2 \times 3) + 4 = \square + 2$

    a. 2
    b. 3
    c. 6
    d. not here

6. $7 \times 4 = 13 + (\square + 15)$

    a. 5
    b. 4
    c. 7
    d. not here

EXERCISE # 3 – Solve the equation. Choose the best answer.

1. $15 + y = 22$

    a. 7
    b. 3
    c. 37
    d. not here

2. $23 - t = 9$

    a. 32
    b. 9
    c. 14
    d. not here

3. $r \times 3 = 33$

    a. 3
    b. 10
    c. 11
    d. not here

4. $n \div 5 = 15$

    a. 3
    b. 5
    c. 15
    d. not here

Practice Skill: MATHEMATICAL REASONING

Expectation: Analyze a math problem and apply an appropriate problem solving strategy.

Tip: The exercises in this section will give you practice in using problem solving strategies.
1. Read the problem as many times as you need to, in order to understand the information given and what question you must ask and solve.
   Draw a picture, diagram, or chart of the information.
2. Identify relevant information and disregard the irrelevant information.
3. Determine what operations you will use to answer the question. Look for key words (total, less than, difference, more than, sum, etc.).
4. Estimate an answer that would make sense. Perform the calculations and compare your answer to your original estimate. Is your answer logical?

Exercise # 1 – Read each of the following problems. Decide if the information given is sufficient to solve the problem or insufficient. Select from the following choices:

> **a. sufficient information**   **b. insufficient information**

1. The mean temperature in Mammoth Lakes, California for three days last January was 30°F. What was the high temperature during that period?

2. The high temperature in Death Valley, California was 110°F yesterday. The low temperature yesterday was 85°F. What was the difference in the temperature?

3. There are 28 students in Mrs. Johnson's math class. Ten of them walk to school, and one-fourth of them take the bus. Two students ride a bike to and from school. The rest of the students carpool to class. How many students are in a carpool?

4. Susana earned $10 in one month. She spent $5.00. What fraction remains?

5. The length of a rectangular bulletin board is 14 cm. The width is 6 cm. How much ribbon is needed to make a border around the bulletin board?

6. The diameter of a circular parachute is 16 feet. What is its radius?

7. Sylvia stopped to rest 3 times during her ten-mile hike. How much time did she spend resting?

Practice Skill: PROBLEM SOLVING STRATEGIES

Expectation: Make decisions about how to approach problems and then perform calculations to solve the problems.

> Tip: The exercises in this section will give you practice in applying the problem solving strategies and operations that are emphasized in the Content Standards. Use the strategies introduced in the "Mathematical Reasoning" section as you work through the problems. Refer to the "Number Sense" and "Algebra" sections for help with the operations.
>
> As you work through this section, keep your work neat and organized. Separate the calculations for each problem. As you work to solve each problem, label your steps or jot down a word or two to help you follow your train of thought. This will save you time when you revisit the problem to use your calculations to solve another problem or to check your answer.

For each problem, determine if it contains sufficient information to solve it. If not, select choice *d. insufficient information.* If the problem gives sufficient information, solve the problem and select the choice that gives the best answer.

1. On a 5 mile hike, Corey stopped to rest for 5 minutes every half-mile. How long did he rest?

   a. 10 minutes
   b. 25 minutes
   c. 50 minutes
   d. insufficient information

2. Substitute teachers work 6 hours per day for $120. What is the hourly wage?

   a. $20 per hour
   b. $32 per hour
   c. $2.00 per hour
   d. insufficient information

3. Kathy decided to give away her coin collection. She sold 124 coins, then equally divided the rest among her 3 sisters. How many coins had been in Kathy's collection?

   a. 331 coins
   b. 125 coins
   c. 172 coins
   d. insufficient information

4. A 1-pound package of chocolate candies has 48 pieces. 1/6 of them are caramels, 1/3 have nuts, and ½ are either light or dark solids. How many of them are nutty or chewy?

   a. 8
   b. 16
   c. 24
   d. insufficient information

5. Which of the following is <u>not</u> a prime number?

   a. 55
   b. 29
   c. 31
   d. insufficient information

6. A chime on a clock strikes one chime at one o'clock, two chimes at two o'clock, up to twelve chimes at twelve o'clock. The clock will sound one chime every ½ hour. What is the total number of chimes that a clock will strike from 6:00 a.m. to noon?

   a. 63 chimes
   b. 69 chimes
   c. 12 chimes
   d. insufficient information

7. Which number is divisible only by a prime number?

   a. 100
   b. 13
   c. 92
   d. insufficient information

8. Read the clues and find the number:

   The number has three digits.
   The hundreds digit is one-half the tens digit.
   The number is odd.
   The sum of the digits is fifteen.

   a. 438
   b. 843
   c. 483
   d. insufficient information

9. If you start with one whole and you cut the pieces in half repeatedly for three seconds, how many pieces do you have?

    a. two halves
    b. three thirds
    c. four quarters
    d. insufficient information

10. Amal's dog is older than Cara's dog. Mo's dog is older than Amal's. Tyrone's dog is older than Amal's dog but younger than Mo's. What can you say about Tyrone's dog?

    a. It is older than Mo's dog.
    b. It is younger than Cara's dog.
    c. It is older than Cara's dog.
    d. insufficient information

11. Which is the better buy, a 4-oz. box of juice for $.59, or an 8-oz. can of juice for $1.22?

    a. 4-oz. box
    b. 8-oz. box
    c. both cost the same
    d. insufficient information

12. Shevaun has $10 to spend on school supplies. She purchases a pack of pencils for $1.79, a $2.25 pen, a tablet of graph paper for $3.98, and a compass and protractor set. How much change does she receive?

    a. $1.98
    b. $1.98 less the amount of sales tax charged
    c. none, because she did not have enough money
    d. insufficient information

13. Andy's plant and garden shop sells four rose bushes for every gardenia plant. Last month, they sold 48 gardenias. How many rose bushes were sold?

    a. 96 rose bushes
    b. 192 rose bushes
    c. 12 rose bushes
    d. insufficient information

ANSWER KEY
MATH

Whole Numbers
1. C
2. D
3. C
4. B
5. D
6. B
7. B
8. D
9. A
10. C
11. D
12. B
13. D
14. A
15. B
16. D
17. C
18. C
19. D
20. B
21. A
22. B
23. A
24. C
25. B
26. C
27. D
28. A
29. B
30. D
31. C
32. A
33. C
34. B
35. C
36. B
37. B
38. A

Number Sense
1. D
2. D
3. A
4. C
5. C
6. D
7. C
8. B
9. C
10. A
11. B
12. D

Measurement and Geometry
1. C
2. D
3. B
4. C
5. C
6. A
7. A
8. A
9. D
10. C
11. B
12. C
13. D
14. B
15. A
16. C

Statistics and Probability
1. B
2. C
3. C
4. D
5. D
6. C
7. C
8. B
9. C

Fractions and Decimals
1. D
2. C
3. B
4. B
5. D
6. C
7. C
8. D
9. A
10. B
11. C
12. D
13. A
14. C
15. B
16. A
17. B
18. C
19. C
20. A
21. A
22. B
23. B
24. A
25. C
26. D
27. B

Patterns and Relationships
1. B
2. B
3. C
4. B

Estimation
1. C
2. A
3. D
4. D

Algebra and Functions
Exercise # 1
1. A
2. B
3. C
4. D
5. D
6. A
7. C
8. B
9. C
10. A
11. A
12. D
13. C
14. A
15. B
16. B
17. C
18. D
19. D
20. A

Algebra
Exercise # 2
1. C
2. D
3. A
4. B
5. D
6. D

Exercise # 3
1. A
2. C
3. C
4. D

Mathematical Reasoning
1. B
2. A
3. A
4. A
5. A
6. A
7. B

Problem Solving
1. C
2. A
3. D
4. C
5. A
6. B
7. B
8. C
9. D
10. C
11. A
12. D
13. B

NOTICE:

In the fourth grade, students in the United States concentrate on individual state history, as well as geography, national government, and map skills. It is impossible to include all individual state histories. We have included a "Mini State Report" for review of the key elements of the student's state history. Answers will vary.

This is a small part of the overall test, but it is suggested that you review your state's history through your social studies book.

HISTORY - SOCIAL STUDIES
Skill: Latitude and Longitude

Many maps and globes have a grid line system that helps us locate exact locations. Latitude lines run horizontally, parallel to each other. Every latitude line is numbered by degrees. The equator, an imaginary line that divides the world into two sections (Northern Hemisphere and Southern Hemisphere), is located at zero degrees. The North Pole is at 90° north and the South Pole is at 90° south. The vertical lines on the map are called longitude lines. Zero degrees longitude is located in Greenwich, England. This line is called the Prime Meridian. The longitude lines are measured in degrees east and west.

Remember that these grid lines help us read maps and describe locations. They are not real lines that you can touch on the earth. If it is hard for you to remember which lines are which, try this trick. Think of the latitude lines as the rungs of a ladder that you can climb up or down, like "ladder-tude" lines.

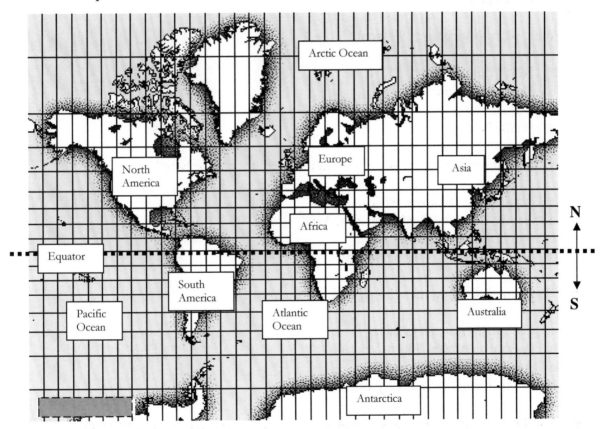

Read the question. Choose the best answer.

1. What is the largest continent south of the equator?

    a. Europe
    b. Australia
    c. North America
    d. Antarctica

2. What map grid line is at 0° latitude?

    a. Prime Meridian
    b. Equator
    c. International date line
    d. North Pole

3. What place is located at 90° south?

    a. North Pole
    b. Prime Meridian
    c. United States
    d. South Pole

4. What continents are located entirely in the northern hemisphere?

    a. Artic Circle, Europe, Africa
    b. North America, South America, Asia
    c. North America, Europe, Asia
    d. South America, Africa, Australia, Antarctica

5. The Prime Meridian runs through the continents of

    a. Europe, Africa, Antarctica
    b. Australia, Africa, South America
    c. Arctic Ocean, Atlantic Ocean
    d. North America, South America, Antarctica

6. The fastest way to fly from Washington, D.C. to the California is to head in which direction?

    a. north
    b. south
    c. east
    d. west

My State Report

Fourth grade standards in History focus on learning more about your home state. One of the best ways to learn about your state is by creating a "Mini-State Report".
You will need an encyclopedia or the Internet to research these questions.

Fill in the following blanks with words and/or pictures.

I live in the state of _____.

Draw an outline of your state.

List all of the states that border your state:

1._____

2._____

3._____

4._____

My state flower is _____

Draw a picture of your state flower.

Draw a picture of your state flag.

What special symbols are on your flag? What do they represent?

_____

_____

_____

_____

_____

Make a timeline of four major events in your state's history.

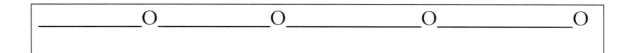

Draw a picture to represent each event.

Make a key for your timeline.

List 5 important people in your state's history. What are they famous

for?

1.

_____

_____

_____

2.

_____

_____

_____

3.

_____

_____

_____

4.

_____

_____

_____

5.

_____

_____

_____

GETTING TO KNOW MY STATE

What is the name of your state capital city?_____

What time zone is your state located in? _____

What special features is your state known for (for example bodies of

water, mountain ranges, or landforms)?_____

_____

_____

_____

What is the population of your state?_____

How did your state get its name? _____

_____

Is there a National Park located in your state?_____

If Yes, what National Park is it? What is special about it?

_____

_____

_____

What is your state motto?_____

What is your state song?_____

_____

What is your state tree?_____

Draw a picture of your state tree:

What is your state bird?_____

Draw a picture of your state bird :

A BIOGRAPHY REPORT

A SPECIAL PERSON IN MY STATE

A special person in my state's history is _____.

This person was born in_____ Died in_____

This person lived in what city?_____

Summarize the life of this special person:

_____

_____

_____

_____

_____

_____

_____

_____

_____

_____

Draw a picture of your special person:

ANSWER KEY
SOCIAL STUDIES

Latitude

1. D
2. B

3. D
4. C
5. A

6. D

My State Report Answers Will Vary.

NOTES

SCIENCE

Practice Skill: EARTH SCIENCES

Expectation: Know basic geology concepts and basic earth science principles.

> Tip: In the earth sciences in the fourth grade, students study the properties of rocks and minerals and how they reflect the processes that formed them. Students also study the various ways that the earth changes: the slow processes, such as erosion; and the rapid processes, such as landslides, volcanic eruptions, and earthquakes. A primary area of focus is how waves, wind, water, and ice shape and reshape Earth's land surface.

Choose the best answer:

1. All rocks are made of tiny crystals called

    a. granite.
    b. minerals.
    c. organic material.
    d. sediment.

2. All minerals are

    a. nonliving things.
    b. living things.
    c. the same color and texture.
    d. poisonous to human beings, even in minute amounts.

3. _____ is the hardest of all minerals.

    a. Talc
    b. Asbestos
    c. Graphite
    d. Diamond

4. In order to identify an unknown mineral, it is possible to conduct a _____ test to see the color that the mineral makes when rubbed across a white surface.

    a. streak
    b. crayon
    c. band
    d. stiffness

5. _____, one of the properties of a mineral, defines the way light bounces off the mineral.

    a. Color
    b. Luster
    c. Hardness
    d. Temperature

6. _____ rocks are formed from molten magma from the center of the earth.

    a. Igneous
    b. Liquideous
    c. Sedimentary
    d. none of the above

7. _____ rocks are formed when grains of rocks are settled with the remains of animals and plants, and after years of being buried, pressed, squeezed and cemented by minerals, they form this substance.

    a. Igneous
    b. Liquideous
    c. Sedimentary
    d. Metamorphic

8. _____ rocks are formed when a volcanic eruption or earthquake produces such intense heat or pressure on existing rock, that new rock is formed from the old type.

    a. Igneous
    b. Liquideous
    c. Sedimentary
    d. Metamorphic

9. _____ are examples of igneous rocks.

    a. Shale and limestone
    b. Gold, silver, and diamonds
    c. Marble and slate
    d. Lava and granite

10. _____ are examples of metamorphic rocks.

    a. Shale and limestone
    b. Gold, silver, and diamonds
    c. Marble and slate
    d. Lava and granite

11. A good description of sediment that is one component of sedimentary rock is

    a. volcanic lava.
    b. tiny grains of rock that are deposited by wind or water.
    c. pressure.
    d. none of the above

12. _____ are examples of sedimentary rocks.

    a. Shale and limestone
    b. Gold, silver, and diamonds
    c. Marble and slate
    d. Lava and granite

13. The _____ is a repetitive process through which rocks are changed from one type to another throughout time. In this process, magma forms igneous rocks which later break into small pieces that become sediment for the formation of sedimentary rocks, which can again be melted into magma.

    a. chemical change
    b. mineral transformation
    c. topical transfer
    d. rock cycle

14. _____ are the remains of past living organisms found in sedimentary rocks.

    a. Fossils
    b. Rocks
    c. Shells
    d. Minerals

15. When boulders break down into sand, and parts of mountains are washed away by the rain, _____ has happened.

    a. lightning
    b. crystallization
    c. erosion
    d. precipitation

16. When water enters rocks, freezes, and expands, it can break the rock apart. When cold nights and warm days cause rocks to expand and contract, the same thing can happen. These are examples of

    a. mechanical or physical weathering.
    b. chemical weathering.
    c. the water cycle.
    d. biological weathering.

17. Most weathering occurs

    a. 20 feet beneath the earth's surface.
    b. in the ozone layer.
    c. on the exposed rocks and soil on the earth's surface.
    d. in magma and active volcanic eruptions.

18. When a living organism such as a tree root, lichen, fungus, or animal causes a rock to break down into soil or sediment, it is called

    a. mechanical or physical weathering.
    b. chemical weathering.
    c. unorthodoxed weathering.
    d. biological weathering.

19. When limestone or marble statues show weathering, it is most likely the natural result of

    a. mechanical or physical weathering.
    b. chemical weathering.
    c. unorthodoxed weathering.
    d. biological weathering.

20. Examples of rapid, natural events that change landforms are

    a. volcanic eruptions and earthquakes.
    b. erosion and chemical weathering.
    c. biological and chemical weathering.
    d. all of the above

21. Earthquakes are caused when _____ that make up the earth's surface collide, separate, or slide against each other.

    a. deposits and silt
    b. friction faults
    c. continental drift
    d. tectonic plates

22. Which of the following statements is <u>not</u> true?

    a. Most volcanoes are found near the boundaries of tectonic plates where the magma can make its way to the surface of the earth.
    b. An extinct volcano is one that is inactive but may become active again.
    c. Most earthquakes and volcanoes occur on the band of land on the edges of the Pacific Plate. It is called the Ring of Fire.
    d. A seismograph is used to measure the intensity of earthquakes.

Practice Skill: LIFE SCIENCES

Expectation: Know the interactions between plants and animals in the life cycle of the planet.

Tip: The life sciences in grade four focus on how living organisms depend on one another and on their environment for survival. The topics include the characteristics of various ecosystems, food chains, food webs, common producers and consumers, and the distinction between omnivores, carnivores, and herbivores.

Choose the best answer.

1. In a(n) _____, animals and plants interact with each other and with the non-living parts of their environment.

   a. ecosystem
   b. natural balance
   c. food chain
   d. food web

2. The biotic factors in an ecosystem include

   a. living things such as plants, animals, bacteria, and fungi.
   b. nonliving physical things such as soil, rocks, minerals, and water.
   c. nonliving non-physical things such as temperature, wind, and light.
   d. choices *b* and *c* only

3. The abiotic factors in an ecosystem include

   a. living things such as plants, animals, bacteria, and fungi.
   b. nonliving physical things such as soil, rocks, minerals, and water.
   c. nonliving non-physical things such as temperature, wind, and light.
   d. choices *b* and *c* only

4. The largest ecosystem in the world is

   a. the shoreline where the ocean meets the edges of the continents, and tides and waves affect the organisms that live there.
   b. the coastal ocean where sunlight reaches the ocean floor and plankton are plentiful.
   c. the open ocean, with organisms living at each of its levels.
   d. none of the above

5. Examples of freshwater ecosystems are

    a. tropical rainforests and jungles.
    b. lakes, rivers, and wetland.
    c. marshlands, meadows, and wetland.
    d. ponds, swamps, and coastal oceans.

6. Trees, shrubs, and grasses are examples of

    a. producers.
    b. primary consumers.
    c. secondary consumers.
    d. decomposers.

7. _____ make their own food through the process of photosynthesis.

    a. Producers
    b. Primary consumers
    c. Secondary consumers
    d. Food webs

8. Squirrels, butterflies, horses, and rabbits are examples of

    a. producers.
    b. primary consumers.
    c. secondary consumers.
    d. decomposers.

9. _____ are secondary consumers.

    a. Green plants
    b. Herbivores
    c. Carnivores
    d. Omnivores

10. _____ frees nutrients from dead plants and animals, which plants use as nutrients to grow.

    a. The water cycle
    b. Photosynthesis
    c. Biodiversity
    d. Decomposition

11. _____ is essential to start the food chain.

    a. Energy from the sun
    b. Water from the ocean
    c. An omnivore that eats plants and animals
    d. Decaying plant matter

12. When scientists make generalizations about the common elements of particular ecosystems, they group them into

    a. populations.
    b. biomes.
    c. species.
    d. nations.

13. Tropical rain forests of the Amazon and New Zealand, coral reefs of the world's oceans, and the tundra of Alaska, Costa Rica, and Tanzania are examples of

    a. food webs.
    b. biomes.
    c. species.
    d. nations.

14. An example of the interdependence of biotic and abiotic factors in ecosystems is when

    a. plants take in carbon dioxide during photosynthesis and release oxygen during respiration. Animals take in oxygen and give off carbon dioxide.
    b. the number of fish and plants in fresh water depends on the amount of oxygen the water contains, how fast it is moving, and its temperature.
    c. a change in the water pressure, light, temperature, or saltiness of ocean water kills some plants and animals that visit or live there.
    d. all of the above

15. Biodiversity

    a. refers to the variety of species of organisms in an ecosystem.
    b. increases as the size of the ecosystem increases.
    c. is greater in tropical rainforests than in deserts, because rainforests have more varied producers that can support more consumers.
    d. all of the above

16. Which of the following factors presents a threat to biodiversity?

    a. pollution
    b. habitat destruction
    c. introduction of non-native species to a habitat
    d. all of the above

Practice Skill: PHYSICAL SCIENCES

Expectation: Analyze electrical circuits, uses of magnetism, and other power sources.

Tip: In the fourth grade, students of the physical sciences learn that electricity and magnetism are related effects that have many useful applications in everyday life. As a basis for understanding this concept, students will be expected to know the following:

1. how to design and build simple series and parallel circuits by using components such as wires, batteries, and bulbs;
2. how to build a simple compass and use it;
3. that electric currents produce magnetic fields;
4. how to build a simple electromagnet; the various uses of electromagnets;
5. that electrically charged objects attract or repel each other;
6. that magnets have two poles; that like poles repel each other, and unlike poles attract each other;
7. that electrical energy can be converted to heat, light, and motion.

Choose the best answer.

1. The positive charge in an atom is in its _____.

   a. nucleus
   b. molecules
   c. electrons
   d. orbitals

2. The charge on a normal atom is _____.

   a. positive
   b. negative
   c. neutral
   d. always changing

3. Electrons have _____ charges.

   a. positive
   b. negative
   c. neutral
   d. changing

4. When two magnets repel each other, their poles near each other have _____ charges.

   a. common
   b. opposite
   c. equal
   d. static

5. Every magnet has two poles called _____.

   a. north and south
   b. positive and negative
   c. electric and static
   d. push and pull

6. Wherever there are moving magnets, _____ current is produced.

   a. magnetic
   b. static
   c. electric
   d. heat

7. A flow of _____ produces the energy of electricity.

   a. electrons
   b. protons
   c. quarks
   d. neutrons

8. Negatively charged particles move from _____.

   a. positive to negative
   b. negative to positive
   c. uphill to downhill
   d. warm to cold

9. The opposite of a conductor is a(n) _____.

   a. circuit
   b. transistor
   c. semiconductor
   d. insulator

10. _____ is the release of a buildup of electrical charge.

   a. Static
   b. Discharge
   c. Resistance
   d. Conductivity

11. A _____ is made up of electric cells.

   a. circuit
   b. magnet
   c. battery
   d. filament

12. Electrical current is measured in_____.

   a. amps
   b. volts
   c. joules
   d. watts

13. Thermal energy or heat can be transferred by _____.

   a. convection
   b. radiation
   c. direct contact
   d. all of the above

14. An example of a semiconductor is _____.

   a. copper
   b. plastic
   c. silicon
   d. wood

15. An example of a conductor is _____.

   a. copper
   b. plastic
   c. silicon
   d. wood

16. If a light bulb is glowing, there is a _____between it and an electrical source.

   a. break in the circuit
   b. complete circuit
   c. magnet
   d. non-conductor

17. A _____ is designed to stop the flow of electricity in an overload.

    a. fuse
    b. transistor
    c. switch
    d. conductor

18. If a magnet is cut in half, the two cut ends will have _____ poles.

    a. both north
    b. both south
    c. one north and one south
    d. east and west

19. One magnet's north pole will attract another's _____ pole.

    a. north
    b. south
    c. closest
    d. strongest

20. The discharge of electricity from a cloud is called _____.

    a. lightning
    b. static
    c. a shock
    d. rain

21. Electrical energy can be converted into _____.

    a. thermal (heat) energy
    b. light energy
    c. kinetic (motion) energy
    d. all of the above

22. Energy moves in _____.

    a. clumps
    b. waves
    c. a constant stream
    d. wires only

23. A compass uses Earth's _____ to help with navigation.

    a. wind currents
    b. temperature
    c. magnetic poles
    d. curvature

24. An electromagnet can be made by _____.

    a. running current through a coil of wire with an iron core
    b. rubbing a balloon against a wall
    c. letting lightning strike a battery
    d. surrounding a magnet with lots of batteries

25. Common electrical outlets provide _____ current.

    a. active
    b. direct
    c. instant
    d. alternating

26. A battery provides _____ current.

    a. active
    b. direct
    c. alternating
    d. divided

27. Batteries use chemical energy to produce _____.

    a. magnetic energy
    b. electricity
    c. light
    d. atoms

28. Electrical currents that change direction often are called _____.

    a. AC
    b. DC
    c. weak
    d. waves

29. Diagram "A" shows an example of a _____.

    a. complete circuit
    b. short circuit
    c. parallel circuit
    d. open circuit

Diagram A

30. In diagram "A" what would happen if one of the bulbs had a broken filament?

    a. All three bulbs will remain lit.
    b. The other two bulbs will remain lit.
    c. It depends on which of the bulbs it is.
    d. None of the bulbs will work.

31. What kinds of circuits are "A" and "B"?

    a. "A" is parallel and "B" is series.
    b. "A" is series and "B" is parallel.
    c. Both are series.
    d. Both are parallel.

Diagram B

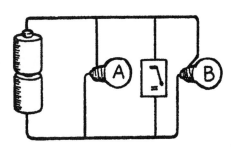

32. Home electrical outlets work like circuit "B." Why?

    a. If nothing is plugged into one socket, the others still work.
    b. It takes less wire to make that kind of circuit.
    c. AC only works if connected that way.
    d. There is no good reason for wiring houses like that.

33. In these circuits, chemical energy is converted to electricity and then _____.

    a. light
    b. sound
    c. chemical energy
    d. all of the above

34. In diagram "C," which bulb(s) will light when the switch is open?

    a. A
    b. B
    c. Both A and B
    d. Neither A nor B

Diagram C

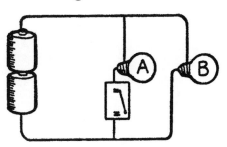

35. In diagram "D," which bulb(s) will light when the switch is open?

    a. A
    b. B
    c. Both A and B
    d. Neither A nor B

Diagram D

36. In diagram "E," which bulb(s) will light when the switch is open?

a. A
b. B
c. Both A and B
d. Neither A nor B

Diagram E

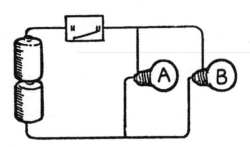

ANSWER KEY
SCIENCE

Earth Sciences

1. B
2. A
3. D
4. A
5. B
6. A
7. C
8. D
9. D
10. C
11. B
12. A
13. D
14. A
15. C
16. A
17. C
18. D
19. B
20. A
21. D
22. B

Life Sciences

1. A
2. A
3. D
4. C
5. B
6. A
7. A
8. B
9. C
10. D
11. A
12. B
13. B
14. D
15. D
16. D

Physical Sciences

1. A
2. C
3. B
4. A
5. A
6. C
7. A
8. B
9. D
10. B
11. C
12. A
13. D
14. C
15. A
16. B
17. A
18. C
19. B
20. A
21. D
22. B
23. C
24. A
25. D
26. B
27. B
28. A
29. A
30. D
31. B
32. A
33. A
34. C
35. B
36. D

NOTES